PUBLIC SPEAKING BASICS

Revised

Michael A. Griffin

University Press of America,® Inc.
Lanham · Boulder · New York · Toronto · Plymouth, UK

Copyright © 2015 by
University Press of America,® Inc.
4501 Forbes Boulevard
Suite 200
Lanham, Maryland 20706
UPA Acquisitions Department (301) 459-3366

Unit A, Whitacre Mews, 26-34 Stannary Street,
London SE11 4AB, United Kingdom

Library of Congress Control Number: 2015930939
ISBN: 978-0-7618-6540-7 (paperback : alk. paper)
eISBN: 978-0-7618-6541-4

Contents

Acknowledgments

I would like to thank Madeline Horinouchi for providing samples of the speaking assignments, as well as Hawley Iseke for reviewing this with an eye toward brevity and sufficiency. I would also like to thank Ms. Joanne Di Lucca Schlub for her repeated editing.

Preface

If students had enough time to cover all the material that is typically found in public speaking textbooks, it would make for more effective speeches. Alas, if a 15-16 week course requiring 5-6 speeches meets three hours per week, approximately one-fifth of the class time is consumed by the performance of the speeches alone. This makes it difficult for an instructor to adequately cover a 200-300 page textbook. Thus, this text will attempt to provide only enough information that can be used within the time constraints of a typical semester. Although the chapters are provided in the given order, instructors should feel free to use them in whichever order they deem most useful or necessary. Further, it is especially useful for instructors to provide video samples of each speech before a class is expected to deliver that speech. Written words and formula are instructive in their own right but audio-visual demonstrations have long been an effective accompaniment.

Students are encouraged to take an argumentation class either before or after taking public speaking to enhance their understanding and skill in the use of reasoning and evidence. This would be especially useful in developing informative and persuasive speeches. In addition, either a voice/articulation or oral interpretation class would provide much-needed emphasis on improved speaking delivery.

CHAPTER 1

Communicating in Public

A. THE NEED FOR SPEAKING

It is not an overstatement that most people do not relish speaking in front of others when they know their speaking will be evaluated, and their public image may be negatively altered on the basis of the perceived quality of that speaking. Not many want to risk that. Yet, our society expects people to speak up since we are considered individuals. If we as individuals, don't speak up for ourselves, who can and will do it for us? We recognize that we naturally have differing ideas about an entire realm of issues that confront us on a daily basis, and we largely consider that any existing differences between us are normal and do not have to be upsetting to harmonious relationships. Further, freedom of speech implies that people need to exercise that right, particularly when they differ in public matters.

Public speaking serves a very important function in that it creates a public, a group of people with some common interests. Its performance is an attempt to coalesce some public in support of some belief or action or event. Much of the public may not even realize their position on an issue of dispute until their hear someone articulate in public arguments for and/or against that issue. In short, people speaking in public help us recognize and understand our own experience and give us additional reasons for accepting and/or rejecting a myriad of ideas. We owe a measure of gratitude to those who are willing to provide a public voice for their and possibly our ideas.

The public speaking class exists to force you, in various speaking situations, to put your ideas and feelings into meaningful and live words directed at an audience in an attempt to gain your desired impact upon this group of listeners. The very skills useful in formal, public speaking are the same communication skills we use throughout our daily life as we communicate with a variety of people (in a variety of contexts), including our person-to-person interactions, organizational situations, and public forums. People need to clarify and organize their ideas, provide logical and emotional reason for holding such ideas, and both descriptively and explicitly communicate these ideas to others in an effective vocal manner. Public speaking skills improve both academic and general communication performance.[1]

B. COMMUNICATION AND THE PUBLIC SPEAKING EVENT

Communication is considered to encompass the simultaneous sending and receiving of messages through one or more channels in some context with some degree of noise present between two or more individuals with some effect on all parties involved.

Public speaking fits this very model of communication. It is one person orally and nonverbally sending messages to an audience which at the same time provides the speaker with at least nonverbal communication messages. They are situated in some context (like a church or public park or classroom), with some degree of noise that interrupts, blocks, or alters the more complete message. Further, there is some impact on those people involved. Since meaning is not in the message but rather in the message user, and given that everyone differs in their physical senses, perception, and personal experience, message receivers will not create exactly the same meaning during the listening process. The challenge for speakers is to gain a sufficiently large overlap in meaning with receivers of the message so there can be a recognition of some understanding between the communicators.

REFERENCES

1. DeVito, J. *Human Communication: The Basic Course*, 10th ed. (Boston: Pearson Education, Inc., 2006).

CHAPTER 1, HOMEWORK #1:
LIKES AND DISLIKES OF SPEAKERS AND SPEECHES

Submit in writing one element that makes for an effective speaking performance and one aspect of some person's public speaking performance that you think is not good.

Your instructor will collect these and use them for a basis of discussion about the many variables in speaking, especially those elements that would make your speeches effective. These may be distributed to the class.

CHAPTER 2

Anxiety about Speaking

A. FEAR OF SPEAKING

Chapter 1 stated that many people fear the act of speaking in public. In evaluative situations almost everyone experiences anxiety. We know that each listener will be critiquing us in addition to the teacher who will be grading us. Further, our self-image and public image will be influenced by the quality of our performance.

We also know that many people who do hear speeches in public often say afterwards that the speeches were boring and a waste of time. We face a tough audience even if fellow classmates don't say anything to us later. Still, if we are to speak, we have to find some way to make our speeches effective.

B. CONTROLLING SPEAKING ANXIETY

A variety of techniques can be used to minimize the impact of any speech anxiety we may have. Like most recommendations, they are easier said than followed.

1. *Think positive.* You should choose a topic you're interested in so you're enthusiasm for it can come out naturally. Feelings are contagious. If you communicate enthusiasm to your audience, they are likely to pick up on that, communicate it back to you, and thus encourage you even more. Some people in advance of their performance specifically visualize themselves doing well during the major parts of the speech. Others find it useful to actually tell themselves they can do it. You are in control of your thoughts so you do not

have to dwell upon making mistakes. In a class situation, students typically want their fellow students to do well.

2. *Be prepared.* If you are not prepared, you have every reason to worry. Being prepared entails the time required to create the speech as well as to practice the delivery of it. Because your appearance is part of your preparation, you may need to dress differently for speeches given *outside* the classroom. If you are prepared, you are likely to have positive thoughts about your impending performance. If you are able to focus on your prepared material as you deliver your speech to your audience, you won't be dwelling on making mistakes

3. *Be realistic about your expected performance.* As much as everyone wants to do well, you cannot expect to be an expert and always perfect when you're taking your first or even second speaking class. You and your peers are likely to be at a similar skill level. You're taking the class to learn and improve. Being anxious is normal, and it can provide motivation to increase your performance level. As you gain experience, your skill level is likely to rise. Challenge yourself to do better with each succeeding speech.

4. *Familiarize yourself with the setting.* This applies to those speaking occurrences held away from your normal meeting place (such as your classroom). Before the speaking event, acquaint yourself with the available lighting, the sound system, the size of the room, the distance to your audience, and the placement of any audio/visual presentational aids. This will allow you to make any necessary alterations in advance. For more rarified occasions, you should probably rehearse the speech in the same room you will present it. Not only will the practice help, but the increased familiarity can allay some nervousness.

5. *Use relaxation techniques.* Take some calming breaths in your seat before you get up to speak. Once up in front, take a slow breath and provide a warm gaze around the room. If it suits you, grab the rear of the podium or lectern that people cannot see to let nervousness channel in that direction as you speak with a calm voice. Take a one-half step to the right and to the left to let some anxiety drain out through your legs. Gaze at but don't concentrate on your listeners' eyes and facial expressions. Consider looking at someone with a smile on their face sitting on the left side of your audience, then swing your gaze to someone with a smile in the middle, then shift your gaze to someone with a smile on the right side, and then repeat the process. This will make it appear you are looking at all of your audience when you are just focusing on a few supportive faces, helping you feel you're dong a good job and thus relaxing you..

CHAPTER 2, HOMEWORK #2:
RECOMMENDATIONS FOR CONTROLLING STAGE FRIGHT

List 2 distinctly different recommendations for reducing or eliminating stage fright while delivering a speech.

Before discussing alternatives for controlling anxiety provided in this chapter, share recommendations in class.

CHAPTER 3

Delivering the Speech

This is the point at which the audience comes in contact with the content of your thoughts and your feelings about them. How you create this transmission will influence the audience's receptivity of your speech. A well delivered speech of average content can be evaluated by an audience as better than a poorly delivered speech with excellent content.

A. VERBAL AND NONVERBAL ACTIONS OF DELIVERY

1. *Eye contact.* An audience wants a speaker to speak to them, not to some notes on a podium (or even to a teleprompter). If listeners are not looked at while they are spoken to, they will typically think about something aside from the speech. If someone doesn't have enough confidence and good will toward the listener to look at whom he or she is speaking to, the listener won't give much credence to what the speaker has to say. Thus, the speaker has to make continual eye contact with the audience, gazing around the group as he or she speaks to them. This requires that the speaker is very familiar with his/her speech material and adept at handling any notes that are referred to during the speech. An added and no less important aspect of eye contact is the receiving of audience reactions to the speech. A flexible speaker can alter what he or she is about to say and even adjust his or her voice to effectively respond to the audience. A speaker can sense a positive regard from the audience that in turn increases speaker energy in delivering the speech.

2. *Conversational style.* To ease the flow of ideas from speaker to listener, speakers should speak to their audience as they would be speaking in a one-to-one basis with their friends during a normal conversation. This will

increase the likelihood of the listener presuming that the speaker is speaking directly to him or her, not at him or her. A normal conversational voice makes the thoughts of the speaker more believable. While people do use incomplete sentences while speaking in one-on-one encounters, be sure to speak in complete phrases or sentences with that personal tone of voice. An added benefit in speaking in a conversational style is that it can be relaxing to the speaker.

3. *Pronunciation.* A speaker's believability will diminish in the audience's mind if the speaker mispronounces words that are spoken. It can seem as if the speaker doesn't know what he or she is talking about. Still, unless the speaker has completed a voice and diction class, he or she won't know how to interpret the pronunciation guide for pronouncing a given word. The speaker should know whether they know a word's correct pronunciation. If there are doubts about a word, the speaker can ask knowledgeable people how they say the word, especially words used in given career field. A separate voice and diction class will provide knowledge and skill in both correctly articulating Standard American Speech sounds and pronouncing words.

4. *Stand up and move.* Speakers need to stand up straight. Slouching over and leaning on the podium conveys a lack of vitality and over-casualness. People won't take you seriously. Keep your hands either at your side or resting on the rear edge of the podium where you can easily move them to make gestures. Never put your hands into your pockets, and jingling of keys and coins is a great distraction. Women should ensure their hair doesn't fall in front of their eyes nor bracelets rap against the podium. While standing, occasionally shift your weight from side to side, alternately taking a one-half step toward the right and then to the left. This conveys energy and helps your blood circulation. Avoid rocking back and forth, which is also distracting.

5. *Gestures.* Moving your hands in a natural-appearing manner can help you emphasize your key points and keep you feeling loose. As you practice at home in front of a mirror, experiment with moving your hands and arms in different ways that compliment what you're saying. This should be done in conjunction with moving your legs and shifting your position towards different parts of the audience. Position your hands on the rear of the podium where they are easily moved as desired.

6. *Vocal Changes.* Speakers need to vary their loudness level, their pitch, and their speed of delivery to communicate their meaning and feeling for that which they are saying. Monotone deliveries are considered boring and listeners will stop listening to the speaker. In advance, practice changing your loudness, pitch, and rate of speech according to the ideas you are presenting,

as a way to emphasize them. Listen to yourself, tape record yourself, or have a friend or family member listen to you to give you feedback on these. Do you sound alive? Do you sound like you believe in what you are saying?

SUMMARY

Overall, speakers need to convey the idea that they are comfortable in their speaking and can deliver their message in a dynamic manner which aids the audience in both understanding and acceptance of the speaker's thoughts.

B. METHODS OF DELIVERY

There are a variety of speech script forms to use when presenting a speech. ranging from no use of notes to speech notes written out word for word.

1. *Impromptu.* In this situation, the speaker uses no notes nor has any preparation and speaks immediately on some topic. This is sometimes termed speaking "off the cuff." It is not uncommon for a student to be called upon in class to briefly speak about a topic under discussion or in the assigned reading. Thinking on your feet is a useful skill. Potential speakers may want to learn about using an introduction, forming a central idea, creating multiple supporting points, use of evidence and reasoning, and how to construct a conclusion to help them effectively present this type of speech. People in a variety of government and business occupations are sought by the media to provide an impromptu (and concise) response about a current issue.

2. *Extemporaneous.* This type of speech should be well prepared for. The speaker would have an outline to follow to ensure that the major sections of the speech are covered—many fill-in words and even some explanations may be omitted on the outline. If the speaker is well prepared, this is the most life-like and seemingly spontaneous of speeches, which audiences are more likely to listen to. With an outline, constant eye contact with the audience, and an accurate reading of the audience response, a speaker can easily adjust the emphasis of his or her speech delivery. This type of speech encourages the use of a conversational voice that appeals to listeners.

3. *Manuscript.* This type of speech preparation requires a great deal of detail to ensure that what a speaker wants to say is written down in just the desired way, because it is read from during the speech. This is helpful when there is a time limit and when the speaker has ideas that he/she wants to

convey in just a certain way (especially controversial ideas). The liability of using a manuscript is that the speaker may speak to his/her script as he/she reads it rather than toward the audience. Lack of speaker eye contact will lead the audience to evaluate the speaker negatively and to daydream. Those speakers following this type of preparation have to know the speaking material so well that they can glance at the script and then speak it to the audience.

4. *Memorization.* In this situation, the speaker commits the speech to memory. This could take the form of memorizing every word or memorizing the organization of the main ideas and like the extemporaneous speech, add the words needed to complete the phrases and sentences. It is impressive when speakers speak in an organized, detailed fashion without using notes. The liability of this style of delivery is that the speaker cannot easily adapt to the audience, and such speeches are invariably spoken in a stilted, robot-like manner. They rarely sound conversational or personable and do require a great deal of time to commit to memory. Further, the speaker may forget to say something deemed important.

CHAPTER 3, HOMEWORK #3:
WORD PRONUNCIATIONS

List five words you hear used for which the pronunciation is uncertain to you. From an American Heritage Dictionary (or one specified by your teacher), also write down the pronunciation form of each word.

Your instructor will collect these and write the pronunciations on the board, helping everyone to correctly pronounce the words. The words submitted may be copied and distributed to the class.

CHAPTER 3 EXERCISES:
VOCAL CHANGES AND IMPROMPTU SPEECH:

1. Complete the vocal variation exercises in Appendix G.

2. The instructor may collect an object from each student, put them in a bag, and have students pick something from the bag. Then they will be asked to give a 1-2 minute impromptu speech on that object. Be advised that preceding this exercise, students need to be familiar with creating an introduction, a body of a speech including a main idea with supporting points, and a conclusion.

Subject Selection and Audience Analysis

You have to speak about some subjects. Whether or not you choose your own topic, you are faced with choices. The following factors inform our choices. Keep in mind that effective communication requires that we identify with our listeners and that they identify with us through the speech we deliver. Each of the following factors should be evaluated in terms of the mutual understanding you expect they will create in your listeners upon reception of your speech.

The concepts of *subject selection* and *audience analysis* are combined here since both depend upon each other and inform each other.

A. SUBJECT SELECTION

1. *Speech Purpose.* Is your speech intended to inform, persuade, or satisfy a special occasion? These are the general purposes. Each requires a different approach with different wording. The informative speech is designed to help the audience understand a concept, person, or action. The persuasive speech tries to influence the audience's behaviors—to get them to believe something and to take some action (otherwise you can't know they have accepted the belief). The special occasion speech varies according to the context as it attempts to get the audience to feel good about something or someone. Amongst the available topics, which ones will suit the overall purpose? Notice how many graduation speeches are not about the graduates or graduation?

The purpose of the speech both influences the subject selection and gives the speech a particular orientation.

a. *Inform.* When the primary reason is to help your audience understand and increase their knowledge of a concept, event, phenomenon, or process.

b. *Persuade.* When the primary speech reason is to influence your audience to act. While persuasion includes the attempt to influence someone's beliefs and/or attitudes about a person, place, or thing, a speaker cannot know that the persuasion attempt is successful unless the receiver of the persuasion acts in a manner that suggests a change of belief and/or attitude (even this doesn't actually prove persuasion occurred).

c. *Special Occasion.* These vary in emphasis from promoting good will, to courtesy, to entertaining. Good will speeches function to acknowledge the special characteristics of someone or some phenomena. Although public speaking in general exits to create a community, it is the variations of the speech of good will that really create a shared sense of community. Courtesy speeches attempt to convey good manners and politeness. When the primary reason for speaking is to amuse the audience, the entertaining speech is fitting. This purpose typically exists for after-dinner speeches, club meeting, and class reunions.

While the above general purposes may appear to be distinct and separate from each other, the speaker and audience will usually find an overlap of one or more of them in a given speech. For example, it would be nearly impossible to have an entertaining speech that didn't inform the audience on some topic, and informative speeches often imply persuasion. Persuasive speeches may attempt to get the community to act in concert for its own good and continued existence.

To help the speaker clarify his or her focus within one of the general purposes discussed above, it is recommended that he or she create a *specific purpose.* The specific purpose narrows the topic area down to a particular area. It describes the exact, concrete goal you are attempting to achieve with the audience through the speech. A speaker may want to inform students about the student financial aid available at that college. Another speaker may want to persuade the students to join the student government as a representative. Another student may give a good will speech congratulating the school baseball team for winning the championship. Other examples specific purposes could include: I want my audience to laugh at the mistakes people make during dating, or I want my audience to know the steps to follow when buying a computer, or I want my audience to buy product x (or vote for person a).

You will need to be clear about the specific purpose so it can guide you in choosing what is relevant to your speech. As the material for a speech is gathered, the expectant speaker has to verify that it fits the specific purpose.

At this point in speech preparation, your goal is to create a specific purpose. Still, this purpose may be altered in completing your audience analysis, which follows later.

2. *Speech Occasion.* The speech selection and the occasion are interrelated so they have to be considered in combination. Choose a topic based upon the following criteria:

a. *It fits the occasion.* Each speaking situation encourages the focus on some topics and discourages the discussion of others. What are the expectations of the audience about what may be appropriate topics? A classroom speech may focus on the benefits of student financial aid, a business speech may emphasize the economic ramifications of a proposed law on the organization, a commencement speech often calls attention to the challenges overcome in meeting graduation requirements and what the graduates hope to accomplish in the future, a political candidates pre-election speech at the community center often touts the benefits of electing him or her to office, an after-dinner speech usually avoids either very sad or very serious speeches, and a priest or preacher's sermon in church typically emphasizes a religious orientation to a subject. You, as the speaker, can list a series of suitable topics for the speaking occasion.

b. *You are interested in it.* If you are, you are likely to better prepare for it and reveal your interest in it with your speech delivery. Begin by listing your interests on a piece of paper (see subject selection exercise example).

c. *Your audience is thought to be interested in it.* If they are, they will be more attentive listeners and provide more supportive, nonverbal messages to you during the speech.

The potential subject suits you. After being clear about the purpose of the speech and potential topics that fit that purpose and the occasion, you will have to decide which topic most interests you. Choosing one you are interested in will be motivational for your preparation and delivery. A topic uninteresting to you will show in your nonverbal messages so your audience will form a low opinion of both you and the topic. You will likely notice their boredom during your speech and feel even worse about it.

Start with your own interests. What are you interested in? What do you spend your time reading about and/or discussing with your friends? Which magazine articles attract your attention, which news stories do you read, which television content is most pleasing to you?

Usually, people have to sort through their various ideas to see which one/s they prefer. To aid you in this process, first write down the topic areas of interest. Next, eliminate those you think the audience would not be interested in. You can also eliminate those deemed inappropriate for the occasion or too large in scope. Lastly, the remaining topics need to fit the communication purpose (inform, persuade, good will). Finally, with the topics left over, you will need to word them in a way that both narrows and makes more specific the discussion of them.

SUBJECT SELECTION EXERCISE

If you have a choice in the topic to be discussed, take a blank page, write the purpose of the speech at the top, then below it list about 20 topics that come to your mind (brainstorm) that could fall under (fit) that purpose. Refine that list by crossing off those for which you have little or no interest. You may have topics left on your page like food, cars, education, football, money, or clothes, which as they stand are too general. You'll have to narrow down each one of them. Next to each general topic remaining on your list, list subtopics. Next to food, you might list fiesta food, fast food, and a vegetarian diet. Next to cars, you could list racecars found at the local racetrack or how to buy a car. Next to education, you could list a certain career available to those with a college degree in Psychology or the cost of attending a university. Next to money you could list saving and investing, and so on.

Cars	a) a car	b) drag racing
Boys	a) choosing boyfriends	b) cultural expectations of boys
Girls	a) an ideal girlfriend	b) sports for girls
Sports	a) the benefits of exercise	b) learning teamwork
Fortune	a) careers with good pay	b) the joys of being rich
Family	a) importance of family	b) single parent families
Fiestas	a) fiesta food	b) keeping friendships
Money	a) saving	b) investing
Local Customs	a) family reunions	b) community service
College education	a) psychology degree	b) local university tuition costs

The more specific topics can be used as a basis for later writing thesis sentences to accompany informative speeches.

The potential subject suits your audience. Do you think your audience would be interested in hearing about your topic? If you expect most of them would not be interested in it, then they are unlikely to listen to you.

Subjects that encourage listener attention focus on, amongst others, the listener's financial well being, physical health, general happiness, or security.

Providing a solution to a known problem the audience is facing will also get their attention, as will controversial topics, or those topics that are new or timely.

Now, examine the different subject lists you've drawn up to determine if the criteria fit one or more of the potential speech subjects. Or, ask yourself if any additional subjects might fit the criteria of your interest, the occasion, and the audience's interest.

B. AUDIENCE ANALYSIS

Audience analysis is the studying of the knowledge, attitudes, and interests of the audience to help the speaker tailor his or her message to fit the audience. The speaker needs to ask him or herself: "What audience generalizations can I assume and incorporate into my speech? What can I say that the audience can identify with so it will consider me a credible source?"

The speech has to fit the audience to increase the likelihood that it will be listened to by the audience. This is also termed listener-centered communication. The speech act is fruitless unless the listener can and will receive the message. This places a burden on the speaker to incorporate ideas within the speech that will speak to the range of variables existing within the audience, to both enable the audience to understand the ideas and emotions expressed within the speech and to react favorably to them.

What are the characteristics of your audience that could influence your subject selection and the point of view you would take about the subject? Does their age suggest they would be interested in a speech about taxes on Guam? If the audience were mostly women, would they be more apt to listen to you talk about racecars or about diets? Would your audience be more likely relate to a speech about Holy Week on Guam or about Mormon missionaries? Would seniors in high schools on Guam be more interested in hearing about military careers than would high school seniors in San Francisco? Does the occasion of a big, outdoor wedding on Guam limit what you might effectively talk about while giving a toast to the bride and groom? If you had to speak at a luncheon meeting of building construction executives on Guam, what limited number of topics would likely interest them? Thus, an analysis of your audience will lead you to delete additional topics on your original list, or at least some of the more specific ones you had made. Remember, you want your audience to listen and consider what you have to say.

There are a multitude of audience characteristics to analyze, so the following will discuss some of the more common ones and their potential impact upon the subject selection and support material used.

1. *Age*. Subjects of interest differ among people according to the age of people. For example, college-age students spend little time thinking about the Social Security system or having a sufficiently large retirement nest egg while retirement finances to both those close to retirement and those in retirement are of supreme interest. High school and college students can discuss the latest hit songs and movie actors/actresses while their middle-aged relatives are unlikely to know them. Thus, the age of the listeners provides a clue about their subject interests and the amount of knowledge they have about different topics. While retirement issues are of little concern to nearly all college-age students, it doesn't mean you cannot speak about these issues to people in this age group. You would have to be mindful of the challenge you face to make it interesting and meaningful to them.

2. *Gender*. While men and women are similar in some respects, they differ in others. What do you need to say about the subject that acknowledges these similarities and/or the differences? If your audience is fairly equally divided among college-age men and women, the concerns they have about the subject of job careers are likely to be similar while they will be both similar and different about the types of careers to which they aspire. If your speech is about the steps to becoming a teacher, will your message need to be the same for both males and females? Will you note that elementary education attracts a near-entirety of female teachers while high school attracts a mixture of them? If you were to give a speech about breast cancer, what do you need to say to attract and maintain the interest of male audience members who have, as a group, an extremely small chance of ever contracting such cancer?

3. *Occupation and income*. An audience largely composed of professionals is going to have very different interests and different career knowledge than an audience largely composed of assembly plant employees. Those in professional jobs are likely to expect their own kids to aspire to such jobs, while assembly plant workers probably spend more time discussing union rules, benefits, and job protection. While college graduates, as a whole, earn more than non-college graduates, assembly line workers may earn more than teachers. If you were to speak to an audience comprised of both groups, what would you say about a proposal to build a new high school that would appeal to both of them, and what would you add that would answer specific concerns of each group of audience members?

4. *Religion*. Although a reference to religion can be controversial, religions do provide a great deal of meaning and direction to people across a variety of subjects. If your audience is comprised of a fairly religious group of Protestants,

what could you expect them to know and believe about abortion or birth control? Would an American Catholic audience expect Catholic American politicians to take directions from the Pope? To what extent are both Protestants and Catholics likely to agree on the subject of church-provided charity to poor people? Even if your own religious beliefs are very important for your position on a given topic, can you also find some non-religious justifications to help convince a non-religious audience to recognize the validity of your position on that topic? In general, how might your audience respond to references you might make, or not make, about the subject of your speech?

Overall, your audience analysis ought to provide an idea about the acceptable knowledge or intelligence level of the subject material to be presented. You need to ensure that your general and specific purposes are neither above nor below the comprehension level of your audience across the characteristics just presented.

C. THE OCCASION

The speech occasion also influences the subject selected. The length of the speech should be tailored to the occasion. Students may anxiously hope to hear a 50-minute biology lecture, while graduates and their family members may only want to hear a 5-minute graduation speech. The occasion suggests a suitable range of time that limits the subjects or the depth that may be covered. The time of day the speech will be delivered will suggest that some topics are more suitable than others. People tend to be a little less alert early in the morning and late in the afternoon. Since the occasion for most people to hear a speech is normally at night, the speaker has to make sure that the subject and how it is handled is interesting enough to get and maintain the audience's attention.

Ensure that you can acquire sufficient information about the topic selected and that you can cover it in depth in the speaking time allotted to you.

While the speech occasion may seem to exist to benefit the audience, it also offers at least an equal opportunity for the speaker to educate him or herself further on the topic selected. Which subjects are you interested in learning more? Can you benefit from further exploration?

Effective Length of Speech Time

After narrowing down your general topics to specific ones, you can eliminate other topics as you consider the length of speaking time available for the occasion. How long do you have to speak? If this is for a school assignment, you will have to meet the stated time requirements. Outside of school, you may be given a set block of time. As a general rule, prepare to speak less than the time allotted so as to maximize audience attention and force yourself to limit your speech to just the most important material. If your boss says you have ten minutes, plan to speak for eight; if you are told you have twenty minutes to present a new product or service to a group of people, plan for a 15-minute speech. Never add material to a speech just to meet the minimum time, but rather have so much material to speak about that you are forced to eliminate the least important parts of your material. Evaluate the topics on your list to determine if you have enough material to speak for the minimum amount of time, crossing off those that won't fit the time allotted.

CONCLUSION

To effectively capture the audience's attention and continued interest in your speech, you have to (among other elements discussed throughout this book) tailor your speech to fit your audience. This does not mean you simply say what they want to hear, to but fit what you want to hear into words, expressions, and ideas that they will reflect upon as you deliver your speech. You have to get to know your audience so you can discover what is meaningful and important to them. Since most audiences are composed of mixed groups of people, provide messages that will speak to what they have in common as well as what fits them, individually. You will have to make generalizations but avoid simple stereotyping where possible in most of your speeches.

CHAPTER 4, HOMEWORK #4:
COMMON AUDIENCE TRAITS; INAPPROPRIATE SUBJECTS

1. List the three most common elements shared by the class and explain their relevance to different speaking topics.

2. List three topics you consider inappropriate subject matter for class speeches and explain why.

CHAPTER 5

Creating a Main Idea

The clearer our communication, the less uncertainty about the meaning of our message and the greater the likelihood that the listener will understand our message. Specificity reduces ambiguity. Misunderstanding is much more likely when the words we use to represent our ideas are vague or too general, in which case we are likely to bypass each other with our intended meanings.

Additionally, listeners usually have competing interests for their attention, as well as having the common urge to speak, rather than listen. Thus, listeners want we, as speakers, to get to the point. If we do not, their attention is likely to wander. In more formal, prepared speeches, as well, speakers need to narrow their topic to fit the time constraints. If a broad topic is attempted when time is limited, few specifics are likely to be covered. The result is likely to be a message that the audience already knows or is unenlightened by. Sensing this, listeners are unlikely to pay attention to the speaker.

A. THE THESIS

Speeches need a main idea, or thesis, to focus the speaker's attention on a specific aspect of some phenomenon and with that focus, provide clarity and understanding for the audience.

The thesis is the yardstick by which ideas and information are evaluated and determined to be relevant to a particular speech. It is the foundation of meaning for an individual speech and serves to coalesce the speaker's ideas.

The implication for us as speakers is that we need to force ourselves to be brief, direct, and clear to aid ourselves in capturing and holding our listeners' attention and to effectively convey our ideas. Our ability to use appropriate thesis statements is beneficial for efficient communication for they should be relatively easy to hear and understand.

What is a thesis statement? It is the basic or fundamental idea of the speech that the speaker wants the audience to accept. It is the central point of view of the subject that the speaker will attempt to affirm by his or her evidence and reasoning. The thesis should " ... [capture] the essence of the information or concept you wish to communicate to an audience."[1]

Characteristics. What are the characteristics of a good thesis statement that make it useful for efficient communication? It is briefly worded, contains only one key idea (no compound sentences), clear, a simple declarative statement, purposive (shows an intention or desired effect), direct (not indirect, as in "is not"), designed for audience acceptance (worded to interest the listeners), and avoids figurative language (which does not clearly express ideas).[2,3,4,5] In formal speeches or writing, it should be a complete and grammatically correct sentence. It should not be phrased as a question since questions do not directly express ideas, nor should it be vague, general, or ambiguous. Terms should not be defined therein since they lengthen and complicate the thesis and easily fit thereafter. Avoid referring to "I/me" since it's redundant and can detract both from being purposive and creating a complete thesis statement about the topic. Comparisons lengthen and complicate the thesis, as well as potentially raise two different ideas. Comparisons can be used as defining and/or supporting information later in the speech. Compound phrases, while not necessarily compound ideas, often extend the length of the thesis and detract from its directness. The thesis subject should be placed near the beginning of the sentence, not at the end. While there is no set number of words by which to judge the length of a thesis, 15-20 words is long (consider that the listener has to remember this key statement) and 10 or less is clearly "getting to the point." The appropriate length is influenced by the complexity of the concept being presented.

As previously suggested, using appropriate thesis statements in our conversations is nott merely for the benefit of the listener. Creating them provides an opportunity for the speaker to focus his or her thinking, to refine and sharpen his or her specific purpose regarding the subject.[5] Therefore, "If you are having trouble phrasing your central idea [clearly and concisely], the reason may be that you do not yet have a firm grasp on your [thesis]."[6] Thus, a focus on developing and using correctly worded thesis sentences can be a technique for us to verify our understanding of our thoughts before we attempt to communicate them to others. Further, "[t]he result will be a sharper [thesis] and a tighter, more coherent speech."[7] The process of creating a clear thesis usually crystallizes our thoughts.

B. FINDING A THESIS TOPIC IN SUBJECT SELECTION

Since speakers are unlikely to have a thesis topic readily available to refine and discuss, they will have to sort through their various ideas to see which one/s they'd prefer to speak about. This process is termed *subject selection* and was discussed in the previous chapter. With the topic selected in the process, students will need to word it in a way that both narrows and makes more specific the discussion of it.

On this and the following pages, examples of both poorly written and correctly written thesis sentences are provided, as well as practice sentences to evaluate.

THESIS SENTENCE EXERCISES[8,9,10,11]

(adapted from Barrett (1981), DeVito (2000), Lucas (2001),
and Whitman & Foster (1987)).

Chapter 5, *Exercise A*. After reading the three statements below,

a. note their weakness/es (reflecting the thesis *Characteristics* list in the previous section).
b. notice how they can be rewritten to make them a correct thesis statement.

1. Can I tell you how to ease your airplane check-in and about the great things I did on Hawaii?
   a. weakness: A complete sentence but unclear since it contains 2 different ideas (compound sentence), is phrased as a question, contains a personal pronoun, and is vague in its reference to "great things."
   b. rewrite: It is easy to check-in for airplane departures. Hawaii has many exciting places to visit.

2. Working on cars is for the birds.
   a. weakness: Figurative language (*for the birds*) and not designed for audience acceptance.
   b. rewrite: Being a car mechanic is a very demanding profession.

3. Let me discuss about sports.
   a. weakness: It is ambiguous about sports, unclear about the speaker's intent, ungrammatical with "about," and uses a personal pronoun.
   b. rewrite: Playing high school football may be detrimental to your grade point average.

Chapter 5, *Exercise B*. After reading the statements below,

    a. list their weakness/s.

    b. rewrite them in a correct manner.

1. Bad things happen to your body when you eat a lot of fat

    a. weakness: _____

    b. rewrite: _____

2. The Native Hawaiian quest for tribal recognition is a nutty movement.

    a. weakness: _____

    b. rewrite: _____

3. Problems of fad diets.

    a. weakness: _____

    b. rewrite: _____

4. Giving children an allowance is a good idea.

    a. weakness: _____

    b. rewrite: _____

5. Here are three ways to save energy around the house, one of which, incidentally, may lead to better health, but I'm not sure about the other two.

    a. weakness: _____

    b. rewrite: _____

CHAPTER 5, *EXERCISE C:*
ADDITIONAL WEAK SAMPLE THESIS
SENTENCES TO BE CORRECTED

1. How does indoor soccer differ from outdoor soccer?

2. Calvin Coolidge was a strong advocate of protection of free enterprise in the business sector.

3. The island of Bali is an awesome place for a vacation

4. Paying college athletic-scholars a salary is a good idea.

5. I'll talk on preparing a soufflé.

6. How is life in the fast lane?

C. THE NEXT STEP: SUPPORTING THE MAIN IDEA

Listeners will be not be satisfied with nor fully understand our main idea if we don't provide additional justification for it. This is done by giving them key supporting ideas and information. These should illuminate and demonstrate the validity of the thesis statements we make.

This additional material "... must be structured and integrated in such a way that listeners perceive the whole."[13] Furthermore, primacy must be given to the thesis since it is the thesis that "... controls or determines the ideas that are appropriate within the speech itself."[13]

To accomplish this, those attempting to create supporting points ask questions such as *what, how,* or *why* of the thesis as a way to generate such supporting points.[14] A persuasive thesis in particular needs to answer *why.* If you want to speak about public health, for example, you might create a thesis like: *Guam Public Health provides needed services for senior citizens.* You would then ask yourself: *what* needed services? At this point, you can list ideas that come to you, such as: dental care, medical care, family counseling, psychiatric care, records, immunization, drugs, laboratory, and x-rays.

The following guidelines are provided to evaluate the supporting main points initially created[15]:

- Eliminate those points that seem least important to the thesis
- Combine points having a common focus
- Choose points of most relevance or interest to your audience
- Use 2, 3, or 4 main points
- Word the points in the same (parallel) style (college graduates can ..., college graduates can ..., etc.)
- Verify that your main points do not overlap each other ("... since it is exciting, thrilling, and pleasurable."). They should be separate and discrete. ("... since it is physically dangerous, emotionally traumatizing, and financially costly.").

Added to the above:

- Avoid a single lead-in phrase preceding the supporting points that identically modifies each supporting point ("... since *it is an efficient way to* save money, invest in stocks, and keep track of your financial status."). It shows more insight and typically provides a greater breadth of information to modify each supporting point differently ("... since it is *an automatic way to* save money, an *insightful method for* investing in stocks, and *an efficient manner of keeping track of* your financial status.").
- Avoid an added-on phrase after the final supporting point that seeks to explain each of the preceding points after they have already been made ("... since you can use the bus, a car, or a train *to get to the stores*."). Rather, San Francisco shopping is easy to access since busses criss-cross the Bay Area, multiple automobile thoroughfares connect with The City, and BART trains run every fifteen minutes from Powel Street."
- Ensure each point's connection with the thesis makes sense. If you say, "Engineering is a financially remunerative career, you cannot have a supporting point that says it is *fun*.

Given the thesis *Guam Public Health provides needed services for senior citizens*, you might select the points that focus on *dental care, medical care, and medical social service care*. Combined, it would read: *Guam Public Health provides needed services for senior citizens, such as dental care, medical care, and medical social service care*. Notice that you will use a few words to connect the thesis with the main points. These include examples like: such as, due to, since, because, including, and so on.

CHAPTER 5, EXERCISE D

In *Exercise A*, the poorly written theses were corrected. In this exercise, three reasonable supporting points are added to each thesis.

1. b. rewrite (2 thesis statements): It is easy to check-in for airplane departures. Hawaii has many exciting places to visit.
   c thesis + 3 supporting points: It is easy to check-in for airplane departures by handing in your luggage the night before, limiting carry on items, and having travel documents in order.
   c. thesis + 3 supporting points: Hawaii has many exciting places to visit, including the the Arizona Memorial, Waikiki Beach, and the Ala Moana Shopping Center.

2. b. rewrite: Being a car mechanic is a very demanding profession.
   c. thesis + 3 supporting points: Being a car mechanic is a very demanding profession since ... you must be keep current on maintenance procedures, know existing car parts availability, and be skilled in parts installation.

3. b. rewrite: Playing professional football may be detrimental to your health.
   c. thesis + 3 supporting points: Playing professional football may be detrimental to your health since it can lead to permanent arthritis, create continual back pain, and cause paralysis.

D. EXAMPLES OF THESIS SENTENCES WITH UNACCEPTABLE SUPPORTING POINTS

1. b. Pearl Harbor, north shore, and the Dole pineapple fields are fun places to visit in Hawaii.
   Weakness: Begin the sentence with the thesis subject, followed by the supporting points.
   The points should be parallel, so "north shore" should be replaced with a specific, named place at north shore, such as "Sunset Beach."

2. b. Being a car mechanic is a very demanding profession since mechanics always have to keep up-to-date on how to fix cars, you have to work on cruddy cars in greasy shops, but you might be well paid.
   Weakness: point #1 is not concise, point #2 has 2 ideas and uses vague terms (cruddy, greasy), point #3 isn't parallel with the viewpoint of the 1st two points.

3. b. Playing professional football may be detrimental to your health, since it can lead to injuries, head injuries, and sore muscles.
   Weakness: points #1 and #2 are not parallel and "injuries" overlaps "head injuries," point #3 doesn't fit the thesis since "sore muscles" does not reinforce "detriment" for most sore muscles lead to greater strength and normally feel fine after a rest of 1-2 days so they are not considered an injury (the idea of the other two points).

CHAPTER 5, EXERCISE E

Using the thesis sentences previously rewritten in *Exercise B* a few pages earlier, add appropriate main points. Transfer the rewritten theses from that exercise to here.

1. Poor thesis: Bad things happen to your body when you eat a lot of fat.

    b. rewrite: _____

    c. rewrite, with 3 main points added: _____

    _____

    _____

2. Poor thesis: The Native Hawaiian quest for tribal recognition is a nutty movement.

    b. rewrite: _____

    c. rewrite, with 3 main points added: _____

    _____

    _____

3. Problems of fad diets.

    b. rewrite: _____

    c. rewrite, with 3 main points added: _____

    _____

    _____

4. Giving children an allowance is a good idea.

    b. rewrite: _____

    c. rewrite, with 3 main points added: _____

    _____

    _____

E. WHERE THE THESIS + SUPPORTING POINTS FIT IN

Considering the outline for the speech, the thesis sentence with accompanying main points would fit into it as follows:

A. Introduction, with supporting statements

B. Body
   1. Thesis statement, followed by 3 main supporting points (combined in one sentence)
   2. Definition of terms (if any)
   3. Statement of first main supporting point, with supporting statements
   4. Statement of second main supporting point, with supporting statements
   5. Statement of third main supporting point, with supporting statements

C. Conclusion, with supporting statements

CONCLUSION

Creating and using thesis sentences in both our everyday conversations and in our prepared speeches and writings provide a method for achieving clear and concise messages. These, in turn, increase the likelihood that we will be listened to and understood. We will also be clearer about our own positions since we'll have had to make them clear and concise for others.

REFERENCES

1. Gronbeck, B., German, K., Ehninger, D., and Monroe, A. *Principles of Speech Communication*, Twelfth Brief Edition (New York: HarperCollins College Publishers, 1995), p. 19.

2. Barrett, H. *Practical Uses of Speech Communication* 5th ed. (New York: Holt, Rinehart and Winston, 1981); DeVito, J. *Human Communication: The Basic Course* 8th ed. (New York: Longman, 2000); Lucas, S. *The Art of Public Speaking* 7th ed. (Boston: McGraw-Hill Company, 2001); Whitman, R. and Foster, T. *Speaking in Public.* (New York: Macmillan Publishing Company, 1987).

3. Lucas, op cit.

4. Ibid., p. 92.

5. Ibid., p. 92.

6. Barrett, op cit.; DeVito, op cit.; Lucas, op cit.; Whitman and Foster, op cit.

7. Gronbeck, p. 18.

8. Whitman and Foster, op cit., p. 49.
9. DeVito, op cit.
10. Ibid.

CHAPTER 5, HOMEWORK #5:
THESIS SENTENCES

On another piece of paper, rewrite the following poorly written thesis sentences. Leave room around your sentences to allow instructor comments. If any sentence has two main ideas, create two separate thesis statements and provide three separate supporting points for each of them. You can make up the supporting points but they must sound reasonable, given the thesis sentence you first create.

Review the thesis characteristics provided on the first two pages of this chapter to determine the thesis weakness below. When asserting a weakness, specify the exact wording that is weak. Do not make up your own criteria. Re-examine the weaknesses of the poorly written theses in the chapter that may provide a comparison with the homework sentences.

Added to the complete sentence *thesis:* provide three reasonable, parallel, non-overlapping main supporting points (be concise) written out in a regular sentence form, as in the chapter. Use connecting words like *since, due to, because, including*, etc. between the thesis and the three supporting points.

Avoid using the multiple supporting points as a way of producing a complete sentence (e.g., "Baseball is fun, expensive, and relaxing." First, make a complete sentence statement about baseball then add three supporting points that fit. Although technically correct, students are not challenged if they are allowed to use a number reference in the thesis statements (e.g., "The quality of meat consists of three criteria."). Rather, make a statement about the subject ("The quality of meat can be easily determined.") and then add appropriate supporting points.

1. The benefits of owning land in Hawaii.
   a. Weakness/es?
   b. Create a grammatically complete-sentence thesis on this line (with a period at the end; no supporting points added here).
   c. Copy exactly the complete-sentence thesis from "b" above, placing it here, and add 3 reasonable-sounding supporting points that fit each other and support the thesis idea.

2. If you drive a car fast, bad things will happen to you.
   a. Weakness/es?
   b. Create a grammatically complete-sentence thesis on this line.
   c. Copy exactly the complete-sentence thesis from "b" above, placing it here, and add 3 reasonable-sounding supporting points that fit each other and support the thesis idea.

3. I think that a government-operated investment account could replacement the Social Security program and the government take out a loan to pay off outstanding retirement and tax debts.
   a. Weakness/es?
   b. Create a grammatically complete-sentence thesis on this line.
   c. Copy exactly the complete-sentence thesis from "b" above, placing it here, and add 3 reasonable-sounding supporting points that fit each other and support the thesis idea.

4. When it comes to fats, pork lard (the white, solid rendered fat of a hog) takes the cake.
   a. Weakness/es?
   b. Create a grammatically complete-sentence thesis on this line.
   c. Copy exactly the complete-sentence thesis from "b" above, placing it here, and add 3 reasonable-sounding supporting points that fit each other and support the thesis idea.

5. I'll speak on planning to build a house.
   a. Weakness/es?
   b. Create a grammatically complete-sentence thesis on this line.
   c. Copy exactly the complete-sentence thesis from "b" above, placing it here, and add 3 reasonable-sounding supporting points that fit each other and support the thesis idea.

6. How is life in Australia?
   a. Weakness/es?
   b. Create a grammatically complete-sentence thesis on this line.
   c. Copy exactly the complete-sentence thesis from "b" above, placing it here, and add 3 reasonable-sounding supporting points that fit each other and support the thesis idea.

7. I will convince you that anyone who thinks American's educational system
   is outstanding is crazy.
   a. Weakness/es?
   b. Create a grammatically complete-sentence thesis on this line.
   c. Copy exactly the complete-sentence thesis from "b" above, placing it
      here, and add 3 reasonable-sounding supporting points that fit each
      other and support the thesis idea.

8. Ronald Reagan was a strong spokesman on what was *right on* with the
   country of America.
   a. Weakness/es?
   b. Create a grammatically complete-sentence thesis on this line.
   c. Copy exactly the complete-sentence thesis from "b" above, placing it
      here, and add 3 reasonable-sounding supporting points that fit each
      other and support the thesis idea.

9. President Harding was not a corrupt president like his biographers made
   him appear, even though some of his staff were.
   a. Weakness/es?
   b. Create a grammatically complete-sentence thesis on this line.
   c. Copy exactly the complete-sentence thesis from "b" above, placing it
      here, and add 3 reasonable-sounding supporting points that fit each
      other and support the thesis idea.

CHAPTER 6

Motivational Appeals

To motivate or persuade an audience to listen to and share the speaker's point of view, the speaker has to provide both logical and psychological reasons for doing so. This chapter emphasizes the use of psychological (emotional) appeals in speeches.

People have a whole range of desired states or conditions they would like to have satisfied in their daily lives, including but not limited to some of the more basic ones, such as sufficient food and a place to sleep, physical and financial security, a range of friendships and interactions with others, and a general feeling that they are a worthwhile person.

The relevance of this is that the speaker can point out to the audience how they currently experience or can expect to experience a lack of one of these desired conditions, meaning that they have a need to satisfy the unfulfilled condition. Upon the audience's recognition of something missing in their lives, the speaker then offers answers for satisfying the missing, craved-for element. Thus, motivational appeals are mental conceptions brought to the listener's awareness that, upon recognition, encourage the listener to respond in some manner to satisfy them. The response could be to alter a personal belief or make some behavioral change. For example, people may appeal to your sense of concern for others and your generosity by asking you to donate money to people who are hungry.

A. COMMON MOTIVATIONAL APPEALS[1]

During your audience analysis, determine which psychological features your audience most desires, representing their needs. Rather than state their needs explicitly, discuss the suffering they experience in relation to the need that will make their lack of fulfillment evident to them.

While listeners aren't likely to become self-conscious about being told they seek companionship or creativity, they may feel uncomfortable about obviously seeking conformity, wanting to show off their economic success symbols, or seeking to dominate others. Be circumspect about these.

You want your statements about these needs to lead to anxiety inside the audience from its recognition of what it lacks, so it will then be available to hear your solution to get rid of that tension (satisfy those needs). The following are some common needs that can be referenced (appealed to). These are briefly explained on the following page.

AFFILIATION	ACHIEVEMENT	POWER
Companionship	Acquisition/savings	Aggression
Conformity	Success/display	Authority/dominance
Deference/dependence	Prestige	Defense
Sympathy/generosity	Pride	Fear
Loyalty	Adventure/change	Autonomy/independence
Tradition	Perseverance	
Reverence/worship	Creativity	
Sexual attraction	Curiosity	

Remember that a *need* is an identified lack of something, a recognition that something desired is missing. The speaker hopes that by bringing attention to the audience's needs, an anxiety or tension will arise in the audience that will then be followed by a desire to have the need satisfied. The speaker hopes that the proposed solution to diminish the audience's tension will be accepted and followed by the audience.

One key reason audiences do follow a speaker's solution suggestion/s is that the speaker, by accurately illuminating audience needs, creates in the audience's mind a sense of identification with the speaker. In this event, the audience (typically unconsciously) concludes that the speaker has its good will in mind so it will then listen more favorably to the speaker's solution.

B. COMMON NEEDS EXPLAINED[2]

1. *Affiliation* needs (perceived lack of, desire to satisfy)

   a. *Companionship.* Those who perceive a lack of sufficient friendships and group attachments in their lives or fear loneliness can be influenced by statements such as, "We care about you," and "You're one of the select group to receive this offer."[3]

b. *Conformity*: Those who have a greater need for others to reinforce who or what they are will try more to fit it and be grouped with others. Teachers may stress that "successful students" do such and such (implying that you should, too) while an ethnic group leader may say that "The pare system is part of our culture" so we should accept it.

c. *Deference/dependence*: People in America are taught to respect their elders and those in legitimate positions of authority. Taking this a step beyond the perceived need to be courteous, those who desire to persuade us may attempt to get us to go along with some action simply for deference sake. Speakers may say, "We respect the wisdom of our elders' position on casino gambling" or "All the mayors agree with the Governor," implying that we should, too. Some people even submit to the wishes or opinion of others since the former depend upon the latter for some financial, social, or political reward.

d. *Sympathy/generosity*: Appeals to our sympathy, generosity, and even our guilt are common To get their kids to finish their food, post World War II parents in the U.S. would say, "Think of the poor, starving child in ____." To solicit a donation, a charity might say, "We could not do it without your support."

e. *Loyalty*: People respect those who are devoted to others and/or worthy causes. Many families tell us "Family comes first, so we/you need to ...." Thus, we may have to forego our personal desires to satisfy the group's needs. If we are not loyal, the group may ostracize us.

f. *Tradition*: There is a powerful urge to do or believe in things just because they have existed a long time since they do offer a guide and imply there must have been good reasons for doing so. To convince us to do things, speakers will tell us "That's our culture [so let's continue]" or " ____ company always raises money for the community."

g. *Reverence/worship*: Many people believe there are forces or people larger than or external to themselves that they need to acknowledge and thank. This could include divine worship, hero worship, or organizational worship. Speakers may point out the outstanding performance of someone or group who's effort and achievement benefited us all.

h. *Sexual attraction*: This is a very powerful need so there is an equally strong urge to satisfy it. Either the physical and/or emotional aspects of this may be thought lacking by those receiving your messages. Many products, services, people, and ideas are made "sexy" to increase their perceived value to our self-worth and interpersonal relationships. Although few will admit it, people who buy the sexy product, service, person, or idea accept the idea that having or holding one of these will imbue themselves with sexual attraction: Thus, they drive certain cars, wear particular clothes, use specific colognes, and so on as a means of making themselves more sexually inviting to other people.

2. *Achievement* needs. This group of needs reflects our desire to increase our self-worth and create a favorable public image. Since we can't be sure of how well we're doing in life simply by looking at our own accomplishments, we compare ourselves to others.

   a. *Acquisition/savings*: People seek financial and material rewards to at least satisfy their basic physical needs, and preferably much more. Other people entice us with the prospect of gaining a well-paying job or earning above-average interest on our money. Financial services companies tell us we have to save and invest. Most people have a need to avoid poverty.
   b. *Success/display*: As shown in *The Millionaire Next Door*,[4] many people who display the symbols of economic success are not wealthy. Still, those very symbols are a yardstick by that most people rate others in life. To get those symbols, we will listen to those who will tell us how to be a millionaire, even how to look like one. We will be encouraged to stand out from the crowd, to make our mark.
   c. *Prestige*: The exceptional quality of a job we have done, or a career we've been in or the amount of possessions we have gives us status in our and other's minds. We are told we're worth it, so we should buy the advertised product. For material possessions, we are told to buy the upscale so we will be prestigious. Otherwise, we will appear plain and assume we will be looked down upon.
   d. *Pride*: People like to feel good about themselves and the groups they associate with, especially by an accomplishment or ownership. To heighten our good feeling via association with the object under discussion, someone may say "Proud to be a _____." These words were in songs both before and after 9/11. People do not want to feel left out so they'll often participate in the activity to assume the advertised pride
   e *Adventure/change*: To avoid boredom, heighten the senses (even through risk), and increase their self-esteem, people will seek to test themselves in some new situation. Products and activities are typically associated with nature or the world at large. New foods, new people, new activities, and new places to explore and conquer.
   f. *Perseverance*: To avoid failure, which would damage our private and public image, we are told to keep trying until we succeed because nothing comes easy and that hard work brings success. Many parents have told their kids that the kids will benefit if they are persistent.

g. *Creativity*: To overcome a lack of individuality and low self-esteem, speakers can offer a product or service that purports to use or reflect the uniqueness of the person. Many hobbies are sold this way, as well as more mundane activities like cooking (cook books). The fields of science, music, English composition, speaking, and others put our creativity to work.

h. *Curiosity*: Most people have a sense of wonder or inquisitiveness in at least some things so they may explore them further. This may result in the excitement of discovery, which colleges, for example, advertise as occurring in their majors at their school. The travel industry offers new places to explore as a way of overcoming boredom in our lives.

i. *Personal enjoyment*: Many products and services are sold on the premise that they will overcome the stress and lack of pleasure in our lives. The material and leisure world promise good times in bottled water, alcoholic drinks, restaurants, spas, vacation spots, and so on.

3. *Power* needs. It is normal and not self-centered to seek some control over our lives. Still, some people go to great lengths in an attempt to control others to satisfy their own needs. History is filled with people who sought to control entire countries and even continents. Offers of methods, products, people or ideas to control our environment may be the strongest appeals we face.[5]

a. *Aggression*: To avoid weakness and being controlled by others, we are told to initiate actions against others. We are not to allow anyone to walk over us, but rather assert ourselves and our presumed rights. Use aggression to satisfy any craving for power. Four-by-four pickup trucks are sold to overcome the landscape, and female "power suits" tell the office males the female is bold and assertive.

b. *Authority/dominance*: As with aggression, we don't want to appear as weak, having no backbone, or at the mercy of others. Many people like to brag that they dominated the other team, an authority figure, or a crisis situation. In a dog-eat-dog world, people are sold products, services, people, or ideas that given them an edge.

c. *Defense*: People naturally want to protect themselves, and governments raise the specter of enemies attacking the country as a method for rallying the citizens to the country's defense. Religions give their members information to defend themselves from competing religions. Products are engineered to defend the homeowner from (exert power over) termites, burglars, the weather, and others.

d. *Fear*: Speakers will point out dangers faced by the audience as a way to create fear in them. To reduce or eliminate the fear, speakers suggest actions designed to diminish or prevent the dangers from occurring. Many would-be persuaders raise the specter of a harm but if they use extreme examples, the audience is likely to reject the likelihood of the bad result occurring.

e. *Autonomy/independence*: While people seek group identifications and associations, they also seek personal freedom and self support, especially in a country in which people are supposed to be free and judged as individuals. To avoid the sameness of others and group control, people are receptive to messages like "Do your own thing," and "Don't be a conformist."

The above lists are not exhaustive of peoples' needs but are some basic ones to raise in your speeches to get the audience's attention and motivate them to accept a belief or take some action.

C. USING MOTIVATIONAL NEEDS

Which motivational needs should you refer to in your speeches? This depends on what you discover in your audience analysis: What primary elements does your audience perceive itself to lack? What products, services, people, or ideas exist to satisfy those? Since our needs are at least partially interdependent, you should be able to discover three to four related ones that fit different parts of your audience. Getting a supportive response to the needs you refer to usually require that they not be readily noticeable in your speech nor be conflicting with each other.

1. *Situation*: Selecting a new vehicle. Speakers could raise a number of factors influencing the audience's decision: if the price is expense (success/ display), source of manufacture is sought after (pride), if the vehicle is an SUV (adventure), if the vehicle needs to do heavy work (perseverance), if many experts favor that model (deference/dependence), if the vehicle is fast (aggression), if it has a high crash-test rating (fear), or if it is a go-anywhere vehicle (dominance). Reminder: do not directly state the needs.

2. *Situation*: Paying off college loans. Speakers could recommend that graduates stay focused and work hard to get out of debt (perseverance), guard against those who would try to abuse them (defense), make regular and timely payments despite having low income (pride), pay off the debt so as to not be beholden to the lender (autonomy/independence), look forward to becoming financially independent when loans are paid off (autonomy, personal enjoyment).

For the audience to know the dangers of not paying off their loans, the speaker can initially provide a variety of support. He or she could cite financial aid rules allowing little deviation of repayment. Testimony could be provided about financial aid departments and banks being unfriendly and unhelpful or family lenders making disparaging remarks about the borrowing member living off the family and not making timely repayments. If the student who borrows does not pay family members back, testimony could be given of his or her being called a free loader or being spoiled. Further support about loan difficulties could cite a bad credit report that increases future car and house interest payments. Investigative journalists could be cited about the usury rates being charged to some student borrowers, and financial planners could provide testimony of the harmful results of the high loan rates. A study could be referred to revealing that many graduates live paycheck to paycheck for years after graduation and experience continual stress about the lack of money which effects the entirety of their lives.

D. RAISING A NEED AND SUPPORTING THE NEED RAISED

For an audience to accept what a speaker thinks is a grave situation, the speaker will have to provide evidence of existing harms that show the audience's desires are not being satisfied. The following are provided as examples of potential audience needs and what a speaker could say that reveals the reality of the need.

1. *Self-worth (self-esteem) need.* Most students know that they are not financially independent and they also probably know that others recognize this fact. Their income is typically below the poverty line. They know they are poor, so they lack the self-worth that comes (in part) from being financially independent.

A speaker could illustrate the existence of the self-worth need with the following hypothetical proof,

- Palo Alto, California newspaper article about the high poverty among students attending Stanford University.
- Testimony by a school counselor that students do not feel good about their finances.
- A study showing low self-esteem among college students about their financial condition and the amount of time they dwell upon it.
- Another study showing that nearly everyone judges everyone else (in part) by the perceived person's apparent financial resources.

- Typical messages by adults about their "just being a student" and not being out there "in the real world." The student feels put-down but has to swallow his or her pride.
- Psychologist testimony that the low self-worth creates a social barrier, decreasing the person's circle of friends, social activities, and even their love life (people are not inspired to become friends with someone having low self-esteem).

Motivational appeals a speaker could suggest or imply to the audience for it to overcome the low self-esteem: acquisition/savings, success/display, personal enjoyment, and sexual attraction.

The satisfying of these will also result in higher perceived self-worth for we will know that we have achieved financial independence (acquisition). Others will recognize it so we will receive those acknowledgments (display). We will enjoy spending money according to the criteria we have set (personal enjoyment), and for financially independent males (at least) women find them more sexually attractive (apart from other characteristics). Personal self-worth is acquired by achieving desired goals, so achieving financial independence becomes an act of self-fulfillment.

2. *Acquisition/savings, success/display, pride needs.* These could arise when there are abuses by sources of financial support. Not typically being financially independent, students are not in a position of power for the money needed to pay for ever-increasing college costs. They have to take it from wherever they can get it, even on unfavorable terms (anticipating greater financial rewards in the future).

With the following as hypothetical proof, a speaker could illustrate the existence of abuses by those who might provide students with financial support.

- School financial aid packages allow little room for deviation in satisfying academic requirements and repayment. Sanctions for not closely following the rules are onerous. Testimony that financial aid departments are often unfriendly, unhelpful, uncaring, and illogical. Money is often late, jeopardizing tuition and living expenses. Study revealing wasted student time, errors in computing financial aid, available aid not recommended nor provided, defensive-arousing behavior of financial aid employees, little sympathy and personal understanding.
- Family lenders make disparaging remarks about the borrowing member to other family members and friends, especially if the borrower is behind in repayment. The borrower gets messages like: free-loader, taking advantage, cannot stand on his or her own feet, and maybe they will not pay it back. The borrower feels embarrassed, may get into

arguments with the lender, and may have to do undesirable favors for the lender.

- Bank student loan repayments not strictly followed after the student completes his/her education results in bad credit report, leading to increased car and house loans in the future. Expert testimony stating that on graduating from college, a student may require 6-12 months to get a job, so they initially have no money to begin repayment of the loan. At the first step of their full-time working life they can easily end up with a low credit score before they have even begun to save for a new car. The higher credit risk can mean an additional $1,000 cost on a car loan and $10,000 cost on a house—with the result that cheaper health care is purchased and the person becomes less healthy as they receive less care. This leads to increased long-term health costs. Since the person cannot afford to pay the increased housing costs to live closer to work, additional commute time is needed, costing more car maintenance and decreased family time.
- Lenders often charge usury rates, taking advantage of borrowers. Testimony by someone in the money/bank lending industry, listing rates and total costs. Testimony by financial planner about the harmful results of this. The borrower feels unhappy knowing they have the debt, that they are not in control of their money, they do not feel safe since they live paycheck to paycheck, and there is continual stress about the lack of money with the distress effecting most other areas of their life. Testimony and study by a financial writer.

Motivational appeals a speaker could suggest or imply to students in financial need for them to avoid or overcome the abuse by those who might provide them with financial support: fear (of the bad outcomes occurring), perseverance (stay focused and work hard to either avoid or stay out of debt), defense (against those who'd control the borrower's life), autonomy/ independence (pay off debt so the borrower is not beholden to anyone), pride (at overcoming the present financial difficulty), personal enjoyment (to look forward to upon financial independent).

CONCLUSION

People are highly influenced by emotional appeals. These can be used in combination and with logical evidence. They can be used in all speeches but are linked most closely with those that are persuasive. In general, speakers indirectly refer to what the audience lacks and then attempt to satisfy that perceived lack (or need) with some relevant information or solution.

REFERENCES

1. Gronbeck, B., German, K., Ehniniger, D., and Monroe, A. *Principles of Speech Communication*, 12th Brief ed. (New York: HarperCollins College Publishers, 1995).
2. Ibid.
3. Ibid, p. 239.
4. Stanley, T., and Danko, W. *The Millionaire Next Door* (New York: Pocket Books, 1996).
5. Gronbeck, B., et al., op cit.

CHAPTER 6, HOMEWORK #6: *MOTIVATIONAL NEEDS*

1. a. Bring to class one magazine, newspaper, or printed Internet advertisement that can be viewed by the class, noting the key statements or visually suggestive messages in the ad.
   b. List (separately) the motivational needs being indirectly referred to by the statements or the visual messages (see the list in the chapter).
   c. Briefly state why you think those needs are being used and whether they are effective or not.

2. a. Assume your friend is considering dropping out of college. Write down five separate reasons you would say to convince him or her to stay in college
   b. For each reason, cite the motivational need being indirectly referred to by that reason, including an explanation of that need so it shows you know about which you are speaking.
   c. Briefly explain why you expect the implied needs to effectively convince your friend. This is your friend, so give the situation due thought.

CHAPTER 7

Organizing and Outlining

With many disparate things to say on a topic and little time available to say it, how can a speaker best be understood by the audience? One key factor is the speaker's organization of ideas.

Listeners can more easily make sense of what people say as well as follow the flow of ideas if the message is organized. If a speech is organized it can also be presented in less time. Further, a well-organized speech conveys the idea that the speaker has good sense and listeners will more easily remember what is said.

The challenge for the speaker is to find and follow an overall arrangement that will help both he or she be clear about what they want to say as well as aid the audience in understanding the speaker's message.

A. BASIC SPEECH STRUCTURE

A. Introduction
B. Body of the speech (the focus of this chapter)
C. Conclusion

While this structure provides a general form, it provides little insight about what to do in each of these sections. The structure of the body, or main part of the speech, is expanded in the following. The introduction and conclusion are dealt with in the following chapter.

B. ORGANIZATION OF IDEAS IN THE BODY

There are a number of patterns that can be followed when arranging ideas in the body of the speech. Which one is followed depends on the speech topic and the purpose of the speech.

1. *Chronological Order.* This one is useful when the speaker wants to describe events or processes occurring over time, especially when demonstrating either how to do something or how something works (e.g, the Demonstration Speech). The main points of the subject are put into a sequence according to when they occur. The following provide some examples.

> *a. Historical Period Topic:* Government executive control on Guam under the U.S. Navy.
> 1. U.S. Navy Admirals Oversee Guam, 1898–1951
> 2. Limited Democracy During the Early Years of the Compact 1951–1970
> 3. Guam Elects its own Governors 1970–present

> *b. Construction Topic:* (process) House painting.
> 1. Preparation
> 2. Painting the Large Surfaces
> 3. Painting the Trim
> 4. Cleanup

2. *Spatial Order.* This structure is useful for describing physical places. The main points are arranged according to where they exist. For a speech about islands in western Micronesia or cities in California, they might be ordered thus:

1. Saipan	or	1. Sacramento
2. Guam		2. San Francisco
3. Yap		3. Los Angeles
4. Palau		4. San Diego

Spatial Order Exercise: fill in the following outline spaces:

1.	Gateway Arch
a.	Toronto
b.	United States
2.	Sears Tower
a.	St. Louis
1)	Canada
2)	Chicago
b.	Wrigley Field/Cubs baseball team
1)	Montreal

3. *Topical Order.* This pattern places speech ideas into the basic topical categories that are then sorted into some order. The ordering of topics often allows some speaker flexibility since topic areas may be independent of each other. A speech about the main components of a car could start with the engine or body or suspension or transmission, but there would be some justification for discussing the car engine first since it provides the power, then the transmission which transfers that power to the wheels, then the body, and finally the suspension which provides a smoother ride for the body.

Suppose you wanted to give a speech about cars. What car topics would you discuss and how would you arrange them? First, you would list all the things about cars you might speak about, narrowing down the list to fit the purpose, audience, information availability, personal interest, and time limit. Then you would create an informative speech thesis sentence about that aspect of cars you decided to focus on. Finally, you would want to create and organize the main points about cars that fit your thesis. Main ideas can be generated by asking yourself *what, how,* or *why* in regard to the thesis.

Topical Order Exercise: assume the thesis sentence about cars is: *Buying a car is relatively easy.* List aspects of cars and their ownership that influence people's car-buying decisions:

color	Purpose	insurance	affordability	parts availability
make	Price	2wd/4wd	safety features	used/new condition
mpg	Engine	wheel base	cargo capacity	extended warranty
size	Seating	2/4doors	down payment	transmission type
loan	Loan	mileage	accessories	warranty

Then sort the ideas according to which seem to fit together and which over-arch other ones. The following outline provides one possibility.

1. First Major Point: Affordability
   a. Sub-Point: Price
   b. Sub-Point: Down payment
   c. Sub-Point: Loan

2. Second Major Point: Make
   a. Sub-Point: Model
   b. Sub-Point: Color
   c. Sub-point: Safety features

3. Third Major Point: Accessories
   a. Sub-Point: Power features
   b. Sub-Point: CD player
   c. Sub-Point: Chrome rims

Verify the chosen supporting points fit the thesis and follow from it. Does it make sense? *Buying a car is relatively easy if you determine its affordability, compare its features with your desired make, and verify its advantageous accessories.* If these were the important factors for you, knowing them would make buying a car much easier than not knowing them.

Notice that you are likely to have listed ideas that do not seem to fit the overall structure and that you thought of some more ideas during the organization process that you originally had not. This is typical. Remember that time constraints will limit what you can cover.

4. *Problem-Solution Order.* People spend a great deal of their time discussing problems they face, so this is a useful pattern for describing such problem and then providing solutions for them. The speaker may want to persuade the audience that his or her solution should be accepted.

Overview:
   1. Description of the problem (harms)
   2. Possible solutions
   3. Best solution

Application:
   1. Many Americans are overweight (problems)
      a. Increased heart attacks
      b. Increased diabetes
      c Increased medical costs
   2. Americans can lose weight (solutions)
      a. Diet
      b. Exercise
      c. Supplements

Follow the _____ diet

5. *Causal Order.* A *cause* is an agent or condition that brings about a particular result. It is a stimulus for a given outcome. The object of this pattern is to clarify both the causes and the effects. When people are unhappy with certain outcomes, they seek to alter what is responsible for them (which can be a separate informative speech or even a persuasive speech).

Overview:
   1. Cause/s (present conditions or causes; reasons for)
      a. one specific one
      b. another specific one
      c. another specific one
   2. Effects [of the conditions or causes; adverse effects (typically harms)]
      a. one specific outcome
      b. another specific outcome
      c. another specific outcome

Application:
  1. There are several key factors which account for teen pregnancy
     a. lack of social sanctions against it
     b. peer pressure
     c. government social support services
  2. Effects of teen pregnancy
     a. many single mothers raising kids
     b. increased anti-social behavior in the community
     c. increased tax burden on working people

In summary, these organization formats are for arranging main and sub-ideas in the body of the speech and are always used in conjunction with a separate introduction and conclusion.

C. ORGANIZING THE ENTIRE SPEECH: THE MOTIVATED SEQUENCE

As the chapter initially described, the basic speech structure requires an introduction, then the body of the speech, and lastly a conclusion. In an attempt to tailor the speech toward a given audience, the *Motivated Sequence* was created.[1] By specifying speech duties that both followed an interconnected logical pattern and stimulated a psychological reaction in the audience to act, this sequence helps ensure speaker success in persuading an audience to believe in something and/or act in some desired fashion. In other words, by speaking to the needs of an audience (problems they are experiencing), the speaker maintains audience attention, creates speaker credibility, and primes (motivates) the listeners to seek information that will satisfy their concerns (needs). With that information, they are prepped and stimulated to act.

The basic speech structure	*becomes* (for persuasive speeches)
A. Introduction	A. Attention Step
	B. Need Step
B. Body of the speech	C. Satisfaction Step
	D. Visualization Step
C. Conclusion	E. Action Step

Explanation of The Motivated Sequence Steps

A. Attention Step: Get the audience interested in the speech so they will want to listen.
B. Need Step: Describe how the audience is or will be harmed by some phenomenon.
C. Satisfaction Step: Provide information about ameliorating the harms.
D. Visualization Step: Describe both the good and bad results that can be expected ahead.
E. Action Step: Specify an action/behavior wanted from the audience.

Modification of the Motivated Sequence for Informative Speeches

A. Introduction
   1. Attention Step: Create audience interest in the topic so it will want to listen.
   2. Need Step: Describe how the audience is or will suffer from some phenomenon.
B Body (Satisfaction): Provide information to solve the harms or more depth about them.
C. Conclusion: Give final comments to end the speech.

The Motivated Sequence for persuasive speeches will be discussed further in Chapter 14, and for informative speeches in Chapter 10. One informative example is provided below.

Sample Motivated Sequence Informative Speech Outline

A. Introduction
   1. I could not wait to graduate from high school so I could go to college and learn the wonders of the world. I looked forward to a carefree life of excitement.
   2. Yet, college can be stressful due to competition for grades and majors—leading to poor eating habits, excessive alcohol consumption, and insufficient sleep.
B. Satisfaction Step
   1. Thesis: College life can be successfully managed by maintaining a healthy diet, by exercising regularly, and by sufficiently sleeping.
   2. Definitions (if any)
   3. First major supporting point: Maintaining a healthy diet
   4. Second major supporting point: Exercising regularly
   5. Third major supporting point: Sufficiently sleeping

C. Conclusion
   1. Summary: You can be in overall control of your life in college by maintaining a healthy diet, exercising regularly, and sleeping sufficiently.
   2. Further Thought: College is a wonderful time of your life, an interlude between the demands of high school and the expectations of full adulthood.

D. OUTLINE FORM AND SYMBOLS

The outline of a speech shows its basic parts and their order. The order of the speech parts reveals their relationship to each other and implies their relative importance. Creating a speech outline tests the speaker's knowledge on the topic and provides a tangible representation of ideas for the speaker and/ or instructor to critique in advance of delivering the speech. At a glance, a reviewer can form a sense of the proposed speech. Further, an outline can be used to speak from when actually delivering the speech.

While convention dictates the use of roman numerals (I, II, III, IV, etc.) when listing major headings, they are not used here since their use is cumbersome. Consider how the first major point in the speech body might look in outline form (from the earlier car example):

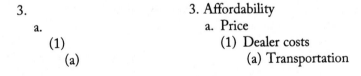

Following the *Motivated Sequence* for informative speeches, the outline symbols might look like (with the accompanying format words):

A. Introduction
   1. Attention Step: Statement
      a. Supporting Statement
      b. Supporting Statement
   2. Need Step: Statement
      a. Supporting Statement
      b. Supporting Statement
B. Body/Satisfaction Step
   1. Thesis
   2. Definitions

3. Statement of First Major supporting point
   a. Supporting Statement
   b. Supporting Statement

[And so on]

E. TRANSITIONS

To help the audience follow the progression of the speech, certain words and phrases can be used between the major sections of the speech and between the supporting points, especially within the body of the speech. These transitional words and phrases act as guides or sign posts, linking the parts of the speech together for both the audience and the speaker. The following are common transitions:

first	however	similar to...	Not only...but also...
second	similarly	nonetheless	Neither...nor...
third	moreover	subsequently	In the final analysis...
since	therefore	in contrast to...	On the other hand...
thus	furthermore	As we can see...	More important than...is...

CONCLUSION

Organization benefits the speaker when arranging the speech and the audience when hearing it. Different organizational patterns fit different types of speeches and purposes. Transitional statements aid in the flow of ideas, keeping the audience on track as it follows the speech. A clear and appropriate organization will also help the audience remember the speech.

REFERENCES

1. Ehninger, D., Gronbeck, B., McKerrow, R., and Monroe, A. *Principles and Types of Speech Communication*, 10th ed. (Glenview, IL: Scott, Foresman and Company, 1986).

CHAPTER 7, HOMEWORK #7: *OUTLINING*

Provide a brief outline example of *each one* of the basic organizational patterns cited in this chapter (chronological, spatial, topical, problem-solution, and cause-effect). Organize the main and sub-points just as the chapter examples illustrate. Choose topics from the following.

Topics: Computer viruses (location, harms, or transmission)
Social Security (history, purpose, or problems)
Single-parent families (history, circumstances, or problems)
Dream interpretation (explanation)
Skin cancer (stages, locations, symptom, or problems)
Fetal alcohol syndrome (stages, location, symptoms, or problems)
Student financial aid (application stages, use of, likely problems)
Dieting (choose one) (steps, reasons, or problems)
Honolulu (or city/state of your choice) (places, activities, education, or problems)
Diabetes (stages, places in the body affected, causes, or problems)

See the following page for an outline form to fill in. Recognize that introductions, conclusions, and thesis sentences are being omitted. A thesis statement will be needed to complete the topical pattern.

CHAPTER 7, HOMEWORK #7:
OUTLINING FORM TO FOLLOW.

Chronological Pattern topic/statement: _____

Historical Order (or)	Process Order
1.	1.
2.	2.
3.	3.

Spatial Pattern topic/statement: _____

   1. _____

      a. _____

      b _____

2. _____

   a. _____

   b _____

3. _____

   a. _____

   b _____

Topical Pattern thesis: _____

1. _____

   a. _____

   b _____

2. _____

   a. _____

   b _____

3. _____

   a. _____

   b _____

Problem-Solution Pattern topic/statement: _____

1. _____

   a. _____

   b _____

2. _____

   a. _____

   b _____

3. _____

    a. _____

    b _____

Causal Pattern topic/statement: _____

1. _____

    a. _____

    b _____

2. _____

    a. _____

    b _____

3. _____

    a. _____

    b _____

Sample Informative Speech Outline Exercise: Find the Organizational Steps *

Directions: In the left-hand column opposite the specific sentences, write in the *Motivated Sequence* organizations steps (by letter, number, and name) for which you find evidence.

Imagine yourself as a thirty-five-year-old parent hearing your 14-year-old daughter say, "Mom/Dad, I think I'm pregnant." You'd be shocked, then probably furious, and finally curious and concerned.

On Guam, teen pregnancy is very high.

My niece had a child at age fourteen, a single parent with no financial income who became a burden on her parents and the taxpayers in the states. She dropped out of high school, on her way to becoming another uneducated adult on Guam, becoming depressed about her situation.

2004 statistics reveal that Guam had 105 teen births per thousand versus a stateside average of 55. Almost all these births become a burden on society. Their offspring are likely to become burdens, too, after being taught the same unproductive life skills.

People in this class are likely to have a single, teenage female relative who becomes pregnant. Your family's financial and emotional support will be sought to help bear the burden.

Adolescents can become educated about parenthood through parental discussions, religious counseling, and government education programs.

Parental discussions provide the foundation for what their children learn about parenthood. They have the opportunity to speak about being a responsible parent with their own child. Children usually trust what their parents say more than what outsiders tell them

Religious counseling provides another avenue to inform teenagers about parenthood. Churches provide youth discussion groups, teen pastor-counselors, and Sunday school classes that speak about parenthood.

Government education programs have existed since the 1960's when schools first began classes on parenthood for middle and high school students. Sex education has been a mainstay of these programs, with students learning about the range of birth control devices.

Teenagers can learn all about becoming a parent through parental discussion, religious counseling, and government education programs.

No parent wants his or her daughter to become a pregnant, single teenage parent. With all the education and options available, there doesn't have to be any accidents.

*Adapted from A. Palomo, 2005.

CHAPTER 8

Introductions and Conclusions

A. THE INTRODUCTION

When you speak, you want your audience to listen to what you have to say. To achieve this, you have to speak to their interests as these relate to the speech topic. It is during the introduction that your audience forms a first impression of you that will influence their reception and perception of the rest of the speech. Make sure your first few sentences are memorized, you look at the audience while you speak them, and you use a full voice. In the speech preparation process, you create your introduction after you have created the body and your conclusion.

Functions of the introduction: gain attention, orient the audience to the topic, and establish credibility. The methods below satisfy one or more of these functions.

Common faults: Do not apologize, rely on gimmicks, or preface your introduction.

METHODS OF INTRODUCTION

1. Personal reference or greeting	4. Illustration (story)	7. Question (rhetorical)
2. Reference to the subject or occasion	5. Humor	8. Presentational aid
3. Startling statement	6. Quotation	

1. *Personal reference or greeting.* Make an interesting comment about your own response to giving the speech, such as being excited about it. You can also extend a warm greeting to the audience, thanking them for providing you the opportunity to speak. If appropriate, you can state your qualifications to speak on the topic.

2. *Reference to the subject or occasion.* You may make an intriguing remark about the subject you will discuss, or a thought-provoking comment about the occasion. You might mention something provocative about how the subject was chosen or how you were chosen to speak.

3. *Startling statement.* By definition, what is said in this instance would have to catch the audience's attention. Some kind of strong or extreme piece of information or point of view would do this. Provide a remarkable or little known but influential fact or statistic.

4. *Illustration.* A brief, detailed, dramatic story. The story should reveal some drama, be relevant to your speech, and in good taste. It would be fitting to tell such a story about audience experiences and/or your own. The story, seemingly over, could again be referred to in the conclusion for its real ending.

5. *Humor.* People love humor, and humor in the introduction immediately sets an audience at ease as well as creating a bond with them. Ensure that the humor fits the subject, occasion, and audience. Do not make a joke just to make a joke, and an ineffective joke at the beginning can almost kill the rest of the speech.

6. *Quotation.* To motivate the listeners to ponder the subject, you can use a catchy quote or one that is consistent with your viewpoint. The quote's source should be respected by the audience. If the audience does not like the messenger, they are very unlikely to accept the message.

7. *Question.* Speakers frequently make rhetorical questions (outward audience responses are not intended) in hope it will encourage the audience to begin thinking about the speech. However easy they are to form, they are often boring so their use should be limited and combined with other methods of introduction.

8. *Presentational aid.* Visual aids, recorded sounds, or even your own style of delivery could get the audience's attention.

B. THE CONCLUSION

It is in the conclusion that the last statements are made, so you will want to use it to reinforce what you have said earlier. To do so, first restate your central idea and the key points so these will be remembered. Then make one last comment, preferably memorable, about the topic. Do not say/ask: "Are there any questions?" Few speaking situations actually allow for this. Further, knowing your topic and your audience, you should have anticipated their questions and answered them during your presentation.

Function of the conclusion: summarize the speech and provide closure. The methods below can be used in combination to satisfy one or both of these duties.

Common faults: Do not apologize, introduce new material, or drag out the conclusion.

METHODS OF CONCLUSION

1. Summary	5. Refer back to what was said in the Introduction
2. Question	6. Refer to (likely) future events
3. Quotation	7. Pose a challenge (persuasion)
4. Statistics	8. State a personal intention (persuasion)

1. *Summary.* Restate the main supporting points, along with the thesis. This is virtually mandatory since speakers want to ensure that these are fresh on the audience's minds after the speech ends. In the conclusion, summarize first and follow it with other methods of conclusion.

2. *Question.* A rhetorical question can also be used in the conclusion. Again, do not be boring and do not use these by themselves. You present a stronger position by declaring what something is than by asking a question about it.

3. *Quotation.* A relevant statement that emphasizes a key idea, stated by a credible source.

4. *Statistics.* These can make a dramatic statement from a brief, numerical fact.

5. *Refer back to what was said in the Introduction.* This can add emphasis to what was earlier said by restatement or can finish a story begun in the introduction, tying the speech together.

6. *Refer to (likely) future events.* This is an attempt to get the audience to envision a likely outcome so the speaker's ideas have some justification. This method is especially useful for speakers wanting to persuade listeners to believe and act on something they have specified. The Visualization Step in the *Motivated Sequence* exits for this purpose.

7. *Pose a challenge.* As an attempt to motivate their audiences to act, speakers will call them to do some action. To simply say "I challenge you" is not very challenging. For it to be meaningful, the speaker will have had to have spoken to the audience's needs, described legitimate solutions, visualized realistic outcomes, and then provided relatively easy and practical actions for success

8. *State a personal intention.* This is another inducement to action, hoping that by you telling the audience what you will do (and possibly by yourself if need be), some of them will follow. Project a strong image, describe a clear path, and say "go" and some people are likely to follow you. You hope people will not want to be left out, will not want to be left behind, or will feel guilty if they do not join you.

CONCLUSION

Use both the introduction and conclusion methods in combination, a minimum of two to three different methods in both the introduction and in the conclusion.

HOMEWORK #8: *TYPES OF INTRODUCTIONS AND CONCLUSIONS*

In the following sample speech, identify at least four different types of introduction methods used and two different conclusion methods used. Clearly write in pen, and large, the number representing your answer next to the start of the sentence being referred to. If multiple sentences are being referred to by a single answer, put a bracket around them and your numbered answer at the beginning bracket. The entire speech is outlined for informational purposes.

Methods of Introduction

1. Personal reference or greeting	4. Illustration (story)	7. Question (rhetorical)
2. Reference to the subject or occasion	5. Humor	8. Presentational aid
3. Startling statement	6. Quotation	

Methods of Conclusion

1. Summary	5. Refer back to what was said in the Introduction
2. Question	6. Refer to (likely) future events
3. Quotation	7. Pose a challenge (persuasion)
4. Statistics	8. State a personal intention (persuasion)

Sample Speech

A. Introduction
   1. Attention step. I walked briskly along Tumon Bay at 6 AM, the pink sunrise filtering through the palm trees onto the glassy water. It was amazing to see so many other people walking or jogging through the warming, slightly salty air. Scores of people in kayaks paddled inside the reef. As Moses liked to say, "It's another gorgeous day in paradise."
   2. Need Step. Unfortunately, people on Guam have significant health-related problem outcomes. My neighbor was overweight and died in his late 50's, leaving his wife and kids traumatized. According to Dr. Nikki Rivera, "Obesity, diabetes, and gout are very prevalent and their symptoms are extremely debilitating." The Annual Guam Physical Fitness Report claimed that 75% of those who are either teenagers or older were found to be in poor physical condition.

B. Satisfaction Step (body)
   1. Thesis. Jogging is advantageous for your physical health, since it leads
      to reduced weight, increases cardio-vascular strength, and enhances
      overall muscle tone.
   2. Definition of terms: none.
   3. Leads to reduced weight.
   4. Increases cardio-vascular strength.
   5. Enhances overall muscle tone.

C. Conclusion
   1. Jogging improves people's overall bodily fitness by bringing about re-
      duced weight, increased cardio-vascular strength, and enhanced overall
      muscle tone. As doctors note, with just 20 minutes a day for 6 months
      at what is a brisk pace for your condition, you will become fit.
   2. As an extra bonus, people have been found to experience a "work-out
      high" when they exert their bodies. Being drenched in sweat just adds
      to the feeling of accomplishment.

**EXERCISE: *DEVELOPING AN
INTRODUCTION AND CONCLUSION.***

For the following topic, with the body of the speech outlined, first create an
appropriate conclusion step and then an introduction step.

A. Introduction

_____

_____

_____

_____

_____

_____

_____

_____

_____

_____

B. Body
1. College students can effectively manage their time by setting realistic goals, getting organized, and avoiding procrastination.
2. Terms
3. Setting realistic goals
   a) *realistic* definition
   b) *goals* definition
   c) determining objectives
   d) determining what's attainable
4. Getting organized
   a) making lists of tasks
   b) scheduling time to do each
   c) checking them off on completion
5. Avoiding procrastination
   a) focus each day on what has to be done
   b) avoiding interruptions
   c) completing tasks immediately

C. Conclusion

_____

_____

_____

_____

_____

_____

_____

_____

_____

_____

_____

_____

_____

_____

_____

Supporting and Amplifying Your Ideas

There are two general types of statements used when we attempt to inform or persuade others, whether we are engaged in normal, everyday, informal communication or are delivering a prepared formal speech before an audience: (1) the claims (conclusions) we want our listeners to accept and (2) the justifications (support, proof (stated or implied)) we provide for those claims. The emphasis in this section will be upon the various ways speakers can validate, illuminate, and even heighten their ideas. While people will occasionally understand and even accept without question a speaker's claims, most listeners will usually require some further explication of what they hear so they can better understand the speaker's point of view. They may even want the speaker's ideas substantiated before they will accept them. Further, the speaker may have a reason to magnify his or her ideas, such as to emphasize its importance, increase the likelihood the listener will remember or respond to it, or even to accept the idea. The following methods are commonly used by speakers to achieve these purposes. These methods, which act as evidence for the speaker's conclusions, may complement each other and are often combined.

A. METHODS OF SUPPORT

1. *Statistics* are numerical data which summarize information used to emphasize the state of a certain situation which the speaker thinks is meaningful. The numbers may emphasize how something is small or large, is increasing or decreasing, or how two different phenomenon are similar in size. Figures by themselves tell little so the speaker has to establish their significance. Although the use of statistics gives weight and authority to generalizations,

do not merely cite figures (or even say that "they speak for themselves") but explain their importance. Verify that they are accurate, recent, specific, from a reliable and preferably unbiased source, and drawn from a sufficiently large group (sample) being measured. If exactness is not needed, round off figures to the closest relevant whole number.

2. *Testimony* is the citing of someone's opinion or conclusion about something observed or collected together and could take the form of a *quotation*. The testimony could be from a witness or authority. State how the person is a relevant and reliable witness and/or the basis of their expertise. Opinions do not prove anything since they are interpretations about facts, beliefs, or other states of existence. The best testimony comes from those with firsthand knowledge, who are capable of accurately observing the phenomenon, or who are experts in the subject matter being discussed and whose background qualifications are known and respected. Be careful not to take the source's words out of context, and cite the source of any quotation used.

3. *Examples* are a brief case in point of an event, concept, or occurrence that is used to clarify something and help prove some point, suggesting a representation or pattern of something, while an *Illustration* is a more detailed story of what did or could occur. Both can be either real or hypothetical. Examples can be either detailed or not, depending upon the audience's familiarity with it, and multiple examples may be used as deemed necessary for audience understanding or persuasion. Verify the examples or illustrations are relevant and representative of the situation or idea, and are highly probable if predicted to occur. A *Specific Instance* is a brief reference to something you expect your audience to be familiar with so you do not have to give very much description of the event, person, place, or process.

4. *Comparisons* (analogies) attempt to equate two or more phenomena as a method for determining which one is superior or to increase the listener's understanding of an otherwise unknown phenomenon. On the basis of what is already known about the recognizable or first phenomenon stated, listeners are expected to understand the unknown or second one being cited. The usual outcome is that one product, service, concept, or occurrence discussed by the speaker is deemed more desirous than another. The two phenomena being compared need to be alike in enough significant aspects and the relationship clear to the audience. The relevance of the similarities should exceed the importance of any existing differences. Recognize that no two things are exactly alike and people tend to be indiscriminate in what they compare. *Contrasts* are statements that emphasize the differences between phenomena, those

qualities that set them apart. They help show what something is not. Be sure that at least one of the phenomena is familiar to the listeners, and that the distinctions clearly separate the two phenomena.

5. *Definitions* of a word attempt to reveal the fundamental character of it. Speakers may do this by citing the etymology (origin or derivation) of the word, or by placing it in a class with like phenomena. Words can also be defined by stating what they are not, or by providing an application example (operational definition). *Descriptions* are explanations used to give clarity to a term, concept, process, event, or proposal. Be concise in using these supporting devices so time is not wasted and the audience does not become bored.

6. *Restatement* is the repeating of an idea in different words to help your listeners remember it.

B. APPLICATION OF SUPPORTING ELEMENTS TO A TOPIC

Soybean products provide significant benefits.[1]

1. *Statistics:* U.S. farmers grow just over 50% of the world's soybeans, making it an important export crop. Further, one cup of soybeans provides over 50% of the daily value for protein.

2. *Testimony:* Dr. Madeline Horinouchi, University of Guam Extension Agent: "Soybeans are one of the healthiest and cheapest sources of nutrition in the world for humans and livestock."

3. *Examples:* Soybeans provide protective effects against heart disease, cancer, and osteoporosis and lead to longer life.

Illustration: Imagine having a Type 2 diabetic person in your family who has a meat protein problem. Then you discover that soybean protein and fiber prevents high blood sugar levels.

Specific Instance: Remember the soy burgers served at John Perez's *Welcome Back Party?*

4. *Comparisons:* Soybeans can be thought of as meat that is boneless and without fat. It can even look similar when it is fashioned into hot dogs, burgers, and steak.

Contrasts: Unlike meat which contains saturated fat and cholesterol, soy protein tends to lead to lower cholesterol levels and a lesser amount of diabetes, heart disease, and strokes.

5. *Definitions:* A leguminous plant cultivated in China over 13,000 years ago, its seeds are used as a source of nutrition by both people and animals, and its bush for soil improvement.

Descriptions: Soybeans are edible seeds of green, yellow, brown, or black color, about one-fourth inch wide, that grow in pods on a bush usually standing five feet tall. Soybeans can be found in various forms such as: fresh, dried, as soymilk, nuts, or flour, and processed as tofu.

6. Restatement: Soy products are a very important source of high quality food and a meaningful source of income for U.S. farmers.

C. PRESENTATIONAL SUPPORT MATERIAL: AUDIO-VISUAL AIDS

Audio-visual aids are used to gain attention, maintain interest, and both clarify and reinforce the speaker's ideas. They can make the supporting facts clearer, more vivid, and convincing. They use tools such as the chalkboard, poster paper/board, projectors, and music players and include printed material such as handouts, charts, graphs, diagrams, maps, or pictures, as well as models, special clothing, and actual people or objects.

When considering the use and selection of presentational aids, answer the following:

1. Is the aid necessary for the critical idea to be understood?
2. Is the aid relevant?
3. Is the message of the aid evident?
4. Does the aid reinforce the idea under consideration?
5. Is the aid appealing?

Rules for use of presentational aids:

1. Ensure that the entire audience can easily see it.
2. Ensure that the visual aid is visually appealing (e.g., use vivid colors, not weak pastels).
3. Use few and simple words on it.
4. Put only one idea or one closely related set of ideas on each chart.
5. Do not stand between your listeners and the visual aid.
6. Be sure you can easily handle the visual aid.
7. Do not unnecessarily leave your aid in view when it will otherwise be distracting.
8. Speak to your audience, not simply to your visual aid.

9. Never pass around any material during your speech.
10. Ensure that the time and cost of creating the aid is justified.
11. Do not project text (especially via Power Point) upon the screen simply to read it, or leave it in sight after its initial use.
12. Be prepared with backup equipment and/or parts. Ensure you can change bulbs in the dark and have a flashlight ready.
13. Consider using simplified backup posters in the event a projector or computer fails.

D. FINDING SUPPORT MATERIALS

Look for supporting materials in a variety of places. Expect to gather much more material than you will end up using; for in the process of limiting your speech to fit the thesis and the time constraints, you will disregard the least relevant and least important information.

1. *Yourself.* Make notes of what you know about the topic. What experiences of yours relate to it? What information have you previously gleaned from the Internet, books, magazine, and newspaper articles?

2. *Books, magazines, and newspapers at home.* Scan these for recent, albeit cursory, information about the subject. Examine the contents of the books you have at home which relate to the topic.

3. *Encyclopedia.* These can be useful as a general source. Hard copies can be found in libraries and they are commonly loaded on personal computers.

4. *Internet search.* Use a web search engine such as Google for resources about your subject. Be very clear about keywords and subject categories for you can easily generate more sources of information than you can evaluate or that can be of use to you.

5. *Library books and periodicals.* One advantage of these is that you can quickly scan the table of contents, the index, and chapter material to see if it's of use.

6. *Interview.* Are there available people you can speak with who study or apply the concepts of the subject you wish to address? Can you find any experts or authorities that can quickly give you some insight on your subject? Take good notes and date them. Recording the interview can provide a more accurate account of what is said.

Be sure to take accurate citations of your sources so these can either be stated in the text of your speech or made available as end notes that would allow you to answer questions about sources.

CONCLUSION

It is in both the speaker's and the audience's interests that the speaker provides adequate justification for the conclusions he or she wants accepted. Inaccurate, incomplete, unstated, and/or irrelevant supporting information may initially be overlooked by the audience, but in the long run (at least) it nearly always harms the speaker's credibility.

REFERENCES

1. "The world's healthiest foods." The George Mateljan Foundation, 2001–2007.

CHAPTER NINE, HOMEWORK #9:
DISCOVERING HOW IDEAS ARE SUPPORTED/DEVELOPED

Given the following speech outline, *NEWSTART Program*, write clearly in pen only one number (one answer) at the beginning of each chosen sentence or bracketed sentences your answer to the type of supporting method being used in that sentence or bracket (see the numbered supporting methods below). Find exactly 15 statements illustrating at least 6 different types of methods, not more than 2 of any one method. Only the first 15 numbered statements will be read and graded.

Types of Supporting Methods

1. Statistics	3. Examples	5. Specific Instance	7. Contrasts	9. Descriptions
2. Testimony	4. Illustration	6. Comparisons	8. Definitions	10. Restatement

NEWSTART Program[1]

A. Introduction
   1. Attention Step. The Flores family enjoys an active life on Guam, going snorkeling every weekend. Mr. Flores plays baseball and golf while Mrs. Flores runs 10 miles every other day. Their son plays on 2 soccer teams.

Need Step.

   a. Yet 50% of the Chamorros on Guam suffer from high blood sugar, preventing an active and long life.
   b. Mrs. Guerrero had uncontrolled diabetes with an average blood sugar count of 300. After 10 years, she had 1 foot amputated at age 45, she went blind at 50, and had kidney failure at 60 when she unfortunately died.
   c. 5% of diabetics will have a foot amputated, 5% will go blind, and 10% will have kidney failure by 60 and die. The cost to have 1 foot amputated is about $2,640 and the healing takes months. Lost eyesight inevitably leads to a lost job and the approximate annual income of $25,000. Kidney treatment requires 3 visits/week to the Dialysis Center, and without insurance costs $600/ visit, $1800/week, $7,200/ month, and $86,400/year. At the end, funerals cost $6,000 plus.
   d. Many people on Guam have a poor diet and limited exercise so friends and fellow fellow students are likely to develop diabetes. When there is a financial debt, family members typically have to contribute, giving up income they actually need for their own spouse and kids, as well taking time to take their loved ones to dialysis. Further, according to Seventh Day Adventist physician Dr. Youngberg, "You might have diabetes since it can be genetically inherited and so many people on Guam have it."[2] Thus, the lifestyle and genes on Guam endanger many of us.

B. Body (Satisfaction)
   1. Thesis: NEWSTART reverses diabetes, by decreasing total fats, by increasing dietary fiber, and by ensuring regular exercise.
   2. NEWSTART: an acronym that stands for Nutrition (whole plant-based foods), Exercise (45-60 minutes/day of aerobics), Water (6-8 cups of pure water/day), Sunshine (regular early morning or late afternoon, no intensity nor burning), Temperance (avoid harmful substances and use in moderation good things), Air (regular outdoor recreation with diaphragm

breathing or oxygenation of blood), Rest (regular sleeping & balancing work with relaxation), and Trust (trust in God). This program is offered through the Guam Seventh Day Adventist Clinic.

3. First, NEWSTART works by decreasing total fats. It lowers fat to less than 10 grams/day. This decreases insulin resistance and decreases total calories. High fats such as meat, vegetable oils, fried foods, and excessive sugar are physically unhealthy. Fat consumption raises blood sugar level, which causes diabetes.

4. Second, by increasing dietary fiber. This decreases insulin resistance. When increasing dietary fiber, people are eating nutrient dense food rather than caloric dense food. Increase dietary fiber to lower blood sugar. Nutrient dense foods are plant based whole food. These include fresh broccoli and other green leafy vegetables, whole grains such as brown rice, whole wheat flour, oat bran, all types of beans, nuts, and fresh fruit. In addition to decreasing blood sugar, people will lose weight and reduce risk of complications. Caloric dense foods are processed foods such as white flour, sugar, and fats, which are found in all fast food restaurants.

Lastly, by ensuring regular exercise. NEWSTART mandates this. When exercising, peoples' muscles burn sugar for energy. This reduces blood sugar. By actively exercising 45-60 minutes/day, people will burn fat and calories, lower their insulin level that will make their bodies cells sensitive to recognizing insulin, and lose weight. This will reduce the risk factors and people will feel healthy.

C. Conclusion
1. Summary. Diabetes can be turned back and its symptoms minimized from following NEWSTART, which works by decreasing total fats, increasing dietary fiber, and ensuring regular exercise. People following this will burn more fat, incur a lower insulin level, and feel better.

2. Further thought. This is not a diet but a lifestyle change to create a longer, healthier life. The NEWSTART Program takes a natural approach to bringing about health and decreases the need for medications or surgery.

REFERENCE

1. M. Horinouchi. Unpublished homework/University of Guam, Mangilao, Guam. November 29, 2003.

2. Dr. Wes Youngberg in an interview by M. Horinouchi, Guam Seventh Day Adventist Wellness Center, Harmon, Guam, November 15, 2003.

CHAPTER 9 EXERCISE 1:
CONVINCING SUPPORT INFORMATION.

Directions: Describe what type of support information it would take to convince you that the following claims are true (not that they are). Answer in the space beneath the claims.

1. People on Guam are very generous.

2. Legalized gambling provides an overall economic benefit to those places allowing it.

3. More than just Lee Harvey Oswald was involved in killing President Kennedy in 1963.

4. That female prosecutor is prettier than all the rest vying for the Attorney General position.

5. Every graduate from U.S. colleges should pass a U.S. history course.

6. The legal alcohol drinking age in America should be a uniform 18 years of age.

7. There is virtually no political difference between Republicans and Democrats on Guam.

8. Smoking marijuana has no deleterious effect on our body.

9. The U.S. landed astronauts on the moon beginning in July 1969.

10. U. S. government employees are less productive than private sector employees.

CHAPTER NINE, EXERCISE 2:
IDENTIFYING SUPPORT INFORMATION USED

Directions: Identify the type of support material used: description, explanation, definition, comparison, contrast, example, illustration, specific instance, statistic, testimony, and quotation.

1. Diamonds are rated according to carat, color, and cutting

2. The $.75 that bought 1 Hershey's candy bar in 2005 would have bought 15 of them in 1970.

3. President Clinton said he did not have sexual relations with Monica Lewinsky.

4. Vice-President Cheney donated $7 million dollars to charity; President Bush gave $70,000.

5. The New York Yankees baseball team has the highest payroll cost in professional baseball.

6. Osama Bin Laden is a hero to Muslims in the Middle East since he attacked Western nations.

7. My $50,000 in total retirement savings is equal to the national average.

8. President Reagan's decisive actions quickly won the final stage of the Cold War with Russia.

9. The earth is round. A Continental flight attendant told me.

10. Stock brokers must follow one basic rule: they have to earn money for the firm.

CHAPTER 10

Informative Speeches

The purpose of the informative speech is to provide information. It should provide greater depth and breadth of understanding on the subject than what is known by the majority of your listeners. It should be enlightening, educative, and possibly instructive. It can occur in different speech forms, including lectures, reports, and instructions. It may primarily provide an explanation, a definition, or a demonstration of some phenomenon.

Since this speech is informational, its most important quality is clarity. For clarity, your thesis will need to be simple and direct (see Chapter 5). The organization will have to be clear (review Chapter 7 for the patterns that can be followed, except the persuasive one). The key terms will have to be understood so they may need to be defined. The speech will have to be descriptive and specific (see Chapter 11). You will need sufficient, clear, and relevant evidence to illuminate and validate your two, three, or four main supporting points. To further justify and amplify your main supporting points, vary your use of the types of aids described in Chapter 9. Your listeners will have to aurally identify what you say, so speak loudly and with appropriate pronunciations. Since each audience is different, you will have to tailor your overall message to suit each one's present knowledge on your topic and comprehension level.

The informative speech should also be concrete, filled with facts, descriptions, and names about the specific object, concept, or instance being discussed. The speaker's goal is to stimulate a conception in the listener's mind that is close to the existing reality being referenced. It is fine to use abstract terms for concepts that you have determined your audience already understands. In a six- to eight-minute speech you should not use more than three main supporting points, for you will be unable to provide enough depth that would be informative for your audience.

People learn about new concepts by associating them with what they already know. Speakers can compare and contrast what is new to the audience to what it already has an understanding. Speakers can also give an example or definition for what is new to the audience. Detailed descriptions help listeners recognize something for what it is.

Notice that audience analysis is crucial to conceptually reaching your audience where it is on the subject. Review Chapter 4 as necessary. Being informative to your audience requires that you sufficiently research the audience and the topic. If you have adequately shown your audience that the subject matter impacts their lives, they will more readily listen to the information you provide about their needs, goals, and/or solutions to achieving those goals.

A. ORGANIZATIONAL PATTERNS
FOR INFORMATIVE SPEECHES

(Chapter 7 review, and excluding introductions and conclusions)

1. *Chronological Pattern* (for describing changes or operations over time)

Historical Order	Process Order
a. The early years of the phenomenon.	a. First step in the process
b. The middle years of the phenomenon.	b. Second step in the process.
c. The latter years of the phenomenon.	c. Third (and last) step in the process.

2. *Spatial Pattern* (for describing physical places)

   a. Beginning place or space is discussed
   b. Next closest place or space is discussed
   c. Next closest (and last) place or space discussed

3. *Topical Pattern* (for common subject matter divisions)

   a. Child abuse can be physical
   b. Child abuse can be emotional
   c. Child abuse can be neglect

4. *Problem-Solution Pattern*

    a. Description of the problem (harms)
    b. Possible solutions
    c. Best solution

5. *Causal Pattern*

    a. Present conditions or causes
       i. one specific one
      ii. another specific one
    b. Effects of the conditions or causes (typically harms)
       i. one specific outcome
      ii. another specific outcome

B. MOTIVATED SEQUENCE PATTERN[1]

(this includes the introduction and conclusion steps that were omitted above)

A. *Introduction Step*

1. *Attention Step*: An opening statement to get the audience's attention and give them an idea about the speech topic. Do not begin by saying "My speech is about ...."—this is boring and unorganized. Use an attention-getting technique from Chapter 8. Avoid common mistakes such as: apologizing, prefacing your speech, or a gimmick that does not relate to your topic and the desired perception of it. You will be speaking about topic harms in the next step, so omit here. Begin by referring to a situation going well in relation to the topic.

2. *Need Step*. This is where you speak to the concerns (needs) of your audience so they will want to listen to what you have to say that will satisfy the concerns. State a problem outcome they have, something that is or will harm them, a threat to their money, property, job security, life itself, health, happiness, education, family, and so on. Do not just say that a problem exists, but describe it and show the audience specific ways that the problem hurts them. *Do not* state that they need to know something. Further, do not just say that a harm exists, but describe it, and show the audience specific ways that the problem harms them. Make them feel anxious and uncomfortable about the topic so they will want to hear what you have to say in the body of the speech. Do the following to accomplish this step.

a. Problem Statement: a clear, concise general statement about the *existence of a problem outcome* (not cause).

b. Illustration: a concise, detailed example which shows someone experiencing the problem outcome/s (suffering in multiple ways).

c. Ramification: additional examples, statistics, testimony, visual aid, etc. which show how wide/far/deep/big the suffering is and the extent the audience is or will be suffering.

d. Pointing: a concise reference to the audience that they are part of the group harmed or to be harmed.

B. *Satisfaction Step* (this main step consumes about three-fourths of the speech time).

1. Thesis: a concise, complete sentence of your main idea, to be followed by your major supporting points.

2. Definition of terms (if any of the words in your thesis may be unclear to your audience).

3. Statement of the first major supporting point (idea).

a. Supporting statement (testimony, quotations, examples, statistics, illustrations, definitions, comparison/contrast, restatement, specific instance, personal experience).

b. Another supporting statement.

4. Statement of the second major supporting point.

a. Supporting statement.

b. Another supporting statement.

5. Statement of the third major supporting point

a. Supporting statement.

b. Another supporting statement.

C. *Conclusion* (to wrap up your speech and help your audience remember your thesis and major supporting information).

1. Summary (restate your thesis with slightly altered words conveying the same idea, followed by the major points).

2. Further thought. Final remark about your topic (two-three sentences). Remember to leave the audience in the desired mood. Omit persuasive words such as: remember, you must, do, etc. Avoid common mistakes: adding new ideas, continued speaking, and apologies.

REFERENCES

1. Ehninger, D., Gronbeck, B., McKerrow, R., and Monroe, A. *Principles and Types of Speech Communication*, 10th ed. Glenview, IL: Scott, Foresman and Company, 1986.

HOMEWORK #10

Given the following topics, create complete sentences illustrating a specific purpose for one informative speech and for one persuasive speech for *each* of the four topics provided (eight grammatically complete sentences total). Review Chapter 4 as needed.

1. Fiesta (party) food	3. University tuition increases
2. Use/Abuse of drugs	4. Land use/Return of excess federal land on Guam

HOMEWORK #11

For your Informative Speech you will have to submit an outline of your speech at least one week in advance of delivering that speech, using the *Motivated Sequence* outline form provided below.

MOTIVATED SEQUENCE INFORMATIVE SPEECH OUTLINE

A. Introduction

1. *Attention Step*. Do not mention problems/harms/suffering here, but describe a situation going well that relates to the topic. Be interesting.

_____

_____

2. *Need/Problem Outcomes Step*: Here you have to show the audience that it lacks (has a need for something (such as: safety, physical health, financial security, happiness, career goals, power, etc.) by pointing out problem outcomes that negatively affect it (harms, suffering, such as: crime, death diabetes, job loss, lack of entertainment, high unemployment, increased school costs, injury, etc.). You want the audience to feel that something has to be learned or done due to something they are lacking or will negatively harm them. Follow these steps:

a. Make a general statement about a harm (implying a need to be satisfied) that does or will exist for the audience (i.e., a statement about people suffering).

_____

_____

   b. Provide an illustration that reveals the problem outcomes/harms
      experienced by people.

      _____

      _____

   c. Provide ramifications of the need (the harms) that do or are likely to
      exist (additional illustrations, specific examples, statistics, testimony,
      definitions, visual aids) for your audience. Here on this form only list
      your data.

      _____

      _____

   d. State clearly and directly to the class (audience) how these problem
      outcomes harm them. Be able to tell the audience that it is suffering
      or can be expected to suffer in the future.

      _____

      _____

B. Satisfaction Step: Body of the speech should last about 4 minutes in a 6
   minute speech.
   1. Thesis statement: Provide a grammatically complete sentence first,
      omitting persuasive words like *should*. Then use connecting words like
      since, due to, because, including, etc., followed by three concise, main,
      supporting points.

      _____

      _____

   2. *Definitions of terms*: If there are key terms in the *thesis* only that require
      understanding. Do not define any supporting points here.

      _____

      _____

   3. Statement of *first major point*. State it exactly as it is with the thesis
      above; *precede it* here with a transitional word/phrase.

      _____

      Supporting information: Here on this form only list your data, and pos-
      sibly define terms.

      _____

      _____

4. Statement of *second major point*. State it exactly as it is with the thesis above; *precede it* here with a transitional word/phrase.

_____

Supporting information: Here on this form only list your data, and possibly define terms.

_____

_____

5. Statement of *third major point*. State it exactly as it is with the thesis above; *precede it* here with a transitional word/phrase.

_____

Supporting information: Here on this form only list your data, and possibly define terms.

_____

_____

C. Conclusion
   1. *Summarizing statement*: Restate the thesis with slightly different words having the same meaning, and add the three supporting points stated *exactly* as they were accompanying the thesis and in the Body.

_____

_____

   2. *Further thought/concluding remarks*: Provide here one of the two to three sentences you plan to use in finishing. Omit persuasive words such as: remember, you must, do, etc.

_____

_____

_____

References
   1. _____
   2. _____

SAMPLE INFORMATIVE SPEECH OUTLINE:
*BREAST CANCER**

A. Introduction

   1. *Attention step.* Looking good, Hollywood! People like positive feelings about their health and appearance, in turn radiating these to others who compliment them and are drawn to them. Most women are especially mindful of their appearance.

Need step:

    a. Yet for some women, feeling attractive can be a thing of the past if they develop breast cancer, "...probably the most ... feared disease among American women."[1]

    b. One of my aunts got breast cancer, forcing her to have a breast removed. Leave from work cost $3,000 and her insurance co-pay was $1,500. She thinks she is a freak and sobs in silence. It pains her to vacuum and miss playing with her kids in the ocean.

    c. 274,900 women are likely to be diagnosed in 2006, with 41,000 expected deaths.[2] The traditional "cure," losing a breast, is devastating. Guam 2002: 26 reported cases, 7 died. Herceptin, costing $2,000/week for 1+ years, is only 20-30% effective.[3] "At ... birth, a baby girl has a 1-in-8 chance of [getting] breast cancer at some point [in] her life."[4]

    d. Women by age 18, like those in this class, are at such risk. While men are unlikely to get breast cancer, the females in your lives may well develop it.

B. Satisfaction Step (body)

   1. *Thesis* Women can increase their chances of surviving breast cancer if they discover their susceptibility, get a regular diagnosis, and seek proper treatment.

   2. *Definition of terms*: Breast Cancer—not needed.

   3. *First, discover their susceptibility.*

    a. heredity: 5-10+% of women; ask female family members about family history.

    b. age: high risk over age 50, age 44 for those with heredity breast cancer.

    c. lifestyle factors: diet, exercise weight gain, smoking, alcohol.

4. *Second, get a regular diagnosis.*
   a. self breast exam: once/month, do one week after menstruation for those in menses.
   b. clinical breast exam: once every 3 years age 20-40, once a year thereafter.
   c. mammograms: annually at age 40, younger (maybe at 25) for those with genetic risk.
5. *Lastly, seek proper treatment.*
   a. lumpectomy: removes tumor and some tissue, preserves breast, often with radiation.
   b. mastectomy: removes part or all of the breast, reconstruction option, often radiation.
   c. systematic therapies: chemotherapy, hormone therapy, immunotherapy.

C. Conclusion
   1. *Summary.* Therefore, if they discover their susceptibility, get a regular diagnosis, and seek proper treatment, women can minimize or avoid life-threatening breast cancer.
   2. *Further thought.* Breast cancer is not pleasant to think about but all women are at risk, and there is increased risk since women are living longer. Early detection can save a life, and secondly that self-confidence that compels the interest and admiration of others.

REFERENCES

1. "Baffled by Choices," in *AARP Magazine*, September/October, 2006.
2. "Dear Annie: October is Breast Cancer Awareness Month," *Pacific Daily News*, October 11, 2006.
3. G. Doleno, "Drug Offers Hope for Breast Cancer Patients."*Pacific Daily News*, October 20, 2005.
4. The Harvard Guide to Women's Health. Harvard University Press, 1996.

* revision of 2009 version.

EXERCISE: SAMPLE INFORMATIVE SPEECH OUTLINE TO EVALUATE AND CORRECT: *OBESITY IN CHILDREN.*

Determine what is wrong with the outline provided, then fill in the blank lines on the right side with appropriate information to make it an acceptable outline.

A. Introduction	A. Introduction
1. *Attention Step* Illustration of field trip to Jose Rios Middle School and the recognition of obese kids	1. *Attention Step*
2. *Need Step* (harms the audience can expect) Parents should become aware and be knowledgeable about ways to prevent obesity in their children.	2. *Need Step*

B. *Satisfaction Step* (body of speech)	B. *Satisfaction Step*

1. Why don't children exercise anymore?
  a. Hi-tech electronics for entertainment
  b. Statistics about TV time
	1. *Thesis statement*

	2. Definition of terms (if necessary)
	3. Statement of 1st major point

2. Good nutrition diet
  a. Parents should be aware of proper amounts and nutrients for the child
  b. Child-growing needs
	4. Statement of 2nd major point

	5. Statement of 3rd major point

3. Why obesity happens
  a. Lack of exercise
    1) Shortage of school budget
    2) Competition in schools
  b. Nutritional influence
    1) parents are always on the go
    2) children easily influenced
    3) skipping breakfast
  c. Lack of stable food environment
	C. Conclusion

	1. Summary
	2. Further thought

4. Solutions
  a. Promotion of good exercise
  b. Promotion of good nutrition
  c. Promotion of stable food environment
  d. Doctor evaluxation
  e. Weight reduction
  f. Stabilization of diet	

CHAPTER 11

Wording the Speech

Speaking is a one-time occurrence requiring instant intelligibility. The words chosen by the speaker have to be instantly understood by the audience as they are spoken or their intended meaning will be missed.

This potential liability is partially due to the communication principle that we send messages but meanings are created by each individual in their own mind. Being different people with different experiences and a different vocabulary developed with that experience, we have differing notions about the meaning/s associated with a given word. This aspect of meaning overlaps with the symbolic nature of language. Words are symbols that represent some thing so the symbolic representations in our minds are not exactly the object or concept being referred to. Further, people do not have a perfect match in their minds for words used between themselves.

Thus, speakers have to consider how the listeners will conceptualize the words spoken and then choose those words that will stimulate listener interpretations that are as close as possible (overlap) to what the speaker is thinking. The question for the speaker is, how to frame the message to increase the chance that the listeners will create the desired meaning/s within themselves? In this chapter, the emphasis is on the words chosen for the speech.

Each speaker brings his or her existing vocabulary to the speaking moment. The Public Speaking class is not going to increase very much anyone's storehouse of known words and how they put them together. Still, the individual speaker can reflect upon his or her wording choices and make some educated decisions.

A. GUIDELINES

1. Words have to be simpler than those used in writing. This aids listener comprehension as well as speaker memory and pronunciation. This does not mean that a speaker should never use words conveying broad concepts or of unknown definitions to the audience. Speakers are encouraged to define largely unknown words in the content of the speech so as to educate (uplift) the audience. Speakers can also increase their own vocabulary by searching for words new to them that better fit the concepts about which they are to speak.

2. In general, these simpler words should be as specific and as direct as possible to aid the listeners' understanding. Seek clear language. Slang, by its nature non-standard, abstract, and typically short-lived, is not descriptive. Certain political demands or even legitimate concerns for some listeners' feelings may compel the speaker to be ambiguous and abstract to minimize objections. This should be done cautiously to avoid being labeled indecisive.

3. For those who have or can develop the artful skill, words selected for their imagery can be very effective in conveying the feelings and ideas of the speaker. Vivid language will emphasize descriptions and actions. This also increases the audiences attention during the speech and their later memory of it.

4. Additional clarity can be gained by using exact numbers, accurate descriptions of objects and events, correct source quotations, and the avoidance of jargon. Exact numbers and accurate descriptions make very definite points and imply that you are clear about the concepts and/or people being described. Misquoting a source suggests sloppy preparation or even bias on your part. Jargon is fine for an audience that understands it (such as automobile terms for an audience of mechanics) but unclear and possibly deceptive for use with the general population.

5. Sentences have to be shorter. Use fewer words in a given sentence than you do in writing so the audience can easily follow your ideas. This will also aid you in speaking complete sentences without pausing.

HOMEWORK #12

A slogan is a phrase expressing the aims or composition of some group or candidate. Often it is a repeated phrase in advertising to promote a person, group, product, or service. It could be a rallying phrase for those people supporting a team or cause.

Directions:

1. Write a slogan you have encountered (such as for a political candidate, a cause, a product, a service, a place, an organization, or an event).
2. Describe the imagery the slogan raises in your mind.
3. Provide an evaluation of the effectiveness of the imagery and the slogan itself.

The following examples provide an idea of what to look for. You can choose one of the following if you like.

Political: Delucchi Works (for Senator); Bring the Democrats (or Republicans) back; People First; Will Never Give Up.

Cause: Pro Life; Responsibility, Not Age (for lowering the legal alcohol drinking age to 18).

Product: Moving You Toward Your Dreams; Building For Generations; We Eat Our Own Cooking.

Service: Building Trust When You Need Coverage And Care. (insurance, medical care)

Place: Where (Business X/City Y/Country Z's) Day Begins.

Event: A Game To Remember; The Greatest Moment In Sports.

Organization/team: Geckos By George. (high school sports team)

CHAPTER 12

Special Occasion Speeches

Good Will, Courtesy, Entertain

These speeches emphasize common identities and values that join people together as a group. They promote and strengthen group members' common beliefs and goals, which in turn increases their positive regard of themselves.

The ceremonial speech answers four basic questions: Who are we? Why are we? What have we accomplished? and What can we become together?[1] In focusing on what an individual or group has accomplished, this speech also promotes these actions as a standard for the group to follow in the future.

There are two basic aspects to ceremonial speeches: identification and magnification.[2]

A. IDENTIFICATION

This is the perception among people that they share something in common. The speaker's goal is to illustrate and magnify those beliefs and experiences that he or she jointly holds with the audience. The audience will not feel as one with the speaker and legitimize their being together in that context if the speaker does not promote identification. Identification can be achieved through:

1. *Use of narratives.* This is done by referring to shared past event, including times of difficulty and discouragement, followed by moments of success when members of the group (now hearing the speech) made significant contributions.

2. *Recognition of heroes.* The speaker names those people in the organization or even public who made superior and unusual contributions to the
product or event. Ensure that all deserving people are acknowledged. The
audience has to be able to recognize that those named are deserving.

3. *Renewal of group commitment.* Visualize for the audience the improved
conditions in the future that can be achieved if the group commitment con-
tinues. Challenge them to not be satisfied with the present success, but to
build on that to shape the future to achieve even greater goals.

B. MAGNIFICATION

Enlarge the worth of some person or event by explaining how:

- The person or group had to overcome obstacles
- The accomplishment was unusual
- The performance was superior
- Their motives were pure
- The accomplishments benefited society[3]

Comparison and contrast of events and people's actions can promote
magnification by making the selected features stand out. This magnification
should increase as the speaker moves toward the conclusion (arrange successes
from earlier and smaller ones to later and larger ones).

Save the best stories, the most illuminating details, for the end of the
speech. The impact of the stories should never diminish as the ceremonial
speech reaches the conclusion.

C. TYPES OF SPECIAL OCCASION SPEECHES

There are a variety of ceremonial speeches, including: Speeches of Good Will
(including Introduction), Courtesy (Welcoming, Acceptances, and Toasts),
and Entertaining/After Dinner.

1. *The Good Will Speech.* The purpose of this speech is to increase the listener's appreciation of a person, product, service, or procedure.[4] The speaker
wants the audience to view the subject more favorably. To accomplish this,
the speaker will have to be both informative and persuasive. Emphasize identification and magnification to achieve these.

The occasions of these speeches are symbolic, and the speeches themselves tend to be standardized. Good Will speeches include, but are not limited to, farewells, wedding anniversaries, funerals, fund-raising campaign kickoffs and celebrations, beginning or end of the year events, political rallies, awards banquets, and other celebrations.

The manner of speaking is very important on these occasions. The speaker's tone of voice should be consistent with the context. Anniversaries, funerals, and the beginning of an event or campaign can be formal and even subdued. This doesn't mean there cannot be some humor to aid in the identification and magnification. Levity in a eulogy can also help inspire a positive view of what the deceased experienced and what the future holds for all those present. It also provides an emotional sense of relief. Anniversaries tend to have even more light-heartedness to them to balance the serious appreciation of those being honored.

Be sure that the audience has been sufficiently informed that the work you do or the service you provide is of value to them, that it makes their lives happier, more productive, interesting, or secure in some way.

2. *The Courtesy Speech.* These include welcoming speeches, acceptance speeches, and toasts. At group functions, someone like a supervisor, coach, or announcer typically greets newcomers or visitors. In this way, the group gets to know a little about the strangers, and they are made to feel more welcome and comfortable. Awards acceptances are also pretty common, and those receiving an award usually give a short acceptance speech, thanking the group for the honor as well as giving credit to those who made the achievement possible. Toasts are given at nearly every wedding, usually by the best man and the maid of honor. These express gratitude and admiration for what the subject has done. Toasts may also be given after the completion of negotiations between competing groups, such as foreign countries, in the hope that they will have continued good relations.

3. *The Entertaining/After Dinner Speech.* The After Dinner Speech exists to give pleasure to a group of people after they have eaten. It is humor with a message. Its theme should relate to the purpose of the group's existence. It should not be too serious or substantive in supporting details, as if the speaker is trying to prove a substantive issue. The speaker should also avoid attempts to get the listeners to reconsider their values or significantly change their beliefs or behavior. Further, this is not a situation to engender anger or negativity. Rather, this speech should help the audience recognize and enjoy their existence, accomplishments, and/or their goals. The after dinner speech should help clarify the group's purpose and encourage it to continue in its efforts.

Humor places people at ease, so it is necessary in most after-dinner speeches. Find humorous stories to tell about the group's experiences, which in the telling create a closer relationship between the speaker and the group.

Not everyone considers him or herself humorous or a joke teller, but anyone can survey group members in advance for funny incidences that have occurred. Groups especially like it when the jokes poke fun at management mistakes that came to no harm. Be careful about offending people, so give humor careful consideration. Don't overlook discussing your comments beforehand with those you are planning to joke about. Speakers may find it safer to joke about themselves as related to the group's activities and purpose. Self-depreciating humor can even increase the audience's perceived credibility of the speaker. Use the humor to make a point, not just humor for humor's sake.

Although stories (real or imagined) are typically used by after dinner speakers, other humorous devices can also be useful, such as puns, witty descriptions and illustrations, humorous lines of poetry, indirect reference (allusions) to famous people or events, and even indirect references to local people and topics. Former President Kennedy was known for using witty comments during his speeches and press conferences. Former President Reagan was known for his Irish jokes and funny allusions to former Hollywood actors and their movie lines, including his own. Although it was not in an after-dinner speech, speaking in the second debate he had with former Vice-President Mondale in 1986, Pres. Reagan said he would not use his opponent's youth as a campaign issue. Even Mondale laughed.

The after dinner speech should have the basic speech parts that include an introduction, body, and conclusion. Get the audience's attention immediately since many in the audience may be talking to other members at their tables or still eating. Use stories to establish a light-hearted mood and to carry a message. Build the stories and comments along a common theme towards the conclusion. Use a brief conclusion that sums up (probably with humor) the overall idea. Remember to be brief, so anything over eight minutes should be considered long and five minutes should be fine.

The following criteria are recommended when creating an after dinner speech:

a. Choose a theme that is suitable to the audience and the occasion.
b. Plan carefully and follow the selected them; avoid irrelevant detail.
c. Develop the theme with appropriate material, being careful to eliminate any that may offend or otherwise distract listeners.
d. Give special attention to transitions, which connect and give coherence to ideas.
e. Use only your kind of stories or humor, that which is easy for you to do.
f. Be brief, especially if in doubt as to the amount of allotted time.[5]

4. *Speech of Introduction.* This type of Good Will speech is given immediately before the featured speaker presents his or her own speech to create in the audience a favorable image of both the featured speaker and his or her message. The introduction is normally delivered by a member of the group that has arranged the speech occasion. To be effective, the introduction speech needs to stimulate a desire in the audience to want to hear the featured speaker. Inform or remind the audience of the speaker's position and accomplishment in the community and/or within the organization. Your role is not to make the expected speech, air your own views on the subject to be discussed by the main speaker, or call undue attention to yourself. You are only the speaker's advance agent and your job is to sell him or her to the audience.

Speeches of introduction help create a friendly relationship between the speaker and the audience, they dispel potential fear about the unknown person (if that is the case) and/or their topic, and they bring about a close feeling between the speaker and the audience.

Two Goals/responsibilities:

1. Arouse the listener's curiosity about the speaker and/or subject.
2. Generate audience respect for the speaker to help his/her message acceptance.

Preparation Steps:

1. Purpose and manner of speaking.
   Know your function. You are providing a service, which is to create for the speaker a position of prominence. You do not want to draw undue attention to yourself.

2. Formulating the content.
   Learn about the speaker, his or her background and biographical data. Arrange a personal interview, if necessary. Be certain all your information is accurate. Know how to correctly pronounce his or her name.

   a. Be brief. As a general rule, saying too much is worse than saying nothing at all. Two to three minutes in length should be sufficient.
   b. Talk about the speaker. Who are they? What is their position in education, business, the community, etc.? Summarize the speaker's primary qualifications to speak on the announced subject but do not overdo it to the point of embarrassment. "Don't bore your audience with a long recital of the speaker's biography or with a series of

anecdotes about your acquaintance with the person."[6] You can use humor but ensure it is in good taste.

c. Emphasize the importance of the speaker's subject and describe how it is relevant to the audience's interests. Only make general comments about the speaker's topic area. Do not praise or blame the speaker's ability as a speaker. Let the speaker emphasize his or her own knowledge and skills.

Organizing the Speech:

1. Use a brief opening to get the audience's attention and interest.
2. Develop 2-3 main points of interest about the speaker.
3. Finish with a key statement about the person and a reference to his or her topic.

For the final statement of your speech, you should make a statement to let the speaker know that the time to speak has come. For example, you might say, "Now to speak to us about _____, Mr./Ms._____" or "Let's give a warm welcome to Mr./Ms._____." After this conclusion, turn toward the speaker and lead the audience's applause.

A sample *Speech of Introduction* is included in Appendix A.

A sample *Special Occasion* speech is provided on the following page and another one in Appendix A.

REFERENCES

1. Osborn, M. and Osborn, S. *Public Speaking*, 2nd ed. Boston: Houghton Mifflin Company, 1991.

2. Ibid.

3. Ibid.

4. Ehninger, D., Gronbeck, B., McKerrow, R., and Monroe, A. *Principles and Types of Speech Communication*, 10th ed. Glenview, IL: Scott, Foresman and Company, 1986.

5. Barrett, Harold. *Practical Uses of Speech Communication*, 5th ed. New York: Holt, Rinehart and Winston, 1981.

6. Gronbeck, B., German, K., Ehninger, D, & Monroe, A. *Principles of Speech Communication*, 12th Brief ed. New York: HarperCollins College Publishers, 1995, p. 284.

HOMEWORK #13

1. For the Speech of Introduction, submit a one to two page biography of yourself one week before the speech is to be given. This can be accurate, partly true and partly fantasy, or entirely fantasy. Your biography will be given to a classmate who will introduce you. They will decide whether to use all, part, or none of what you write down.

SPECIAL OCCASION SPEECH:
GOOD WILL (EULOGY)

Dave's Auto: Closed for Renovation, June 30, 2008.

I first met Dave as he had a 4 o'clock martini at my brother John's house where he gave me an "Ace high and a big Richmond hello." It wasn't 4 pm yet. John said it was 4 pm somewhere. They said they needed a "tune-up" before going to a party, probably at Denny & Mary's. John liked 3 eye-drops of vermouth with his glass of gin. Dave liked them so dry that he simply called up a bar to see if they had any vermouth in stock. The jokes and boasts were flying fast and furious between the two as they pounded their drinks.

I saw him next when he hired me to work at *Dave's Auto* in San Ramon alongside his friend, The Greek. I learned about building VW engines and Indians from Bearcat Creek. I also learned about measuring. Dave normally used feeler gauges to check clearances between car parts, but sometimes he insisted that I know the difference between the thickness of a blond hair and a redhead hair to adjust the gap accordingly. Some parts had to be as close as a "gnats [orifice]." Others were "kyled" or didn't pass the "smell test." Once when I asked him how hard I should tighten down a particular bolt, he replied: "You can't tighten it hard enough." If something was "rode hard and put away wet," well, that wasn't supposed to be good for cars and horses.

On a couple of occasions he enjoined me to take a New Year's day evening lap in his freezing San Ramon swimming pool, followed by a hot tub with Tommy and Jim Beam. Then he had me up to his Occidental property during the winter where the thing to do was to take a scalding hot bubble bath in claw-foot tubs positioned under ferns and redwoods as torrential rain cascaded onto your head, and shout "Herrrr—maaann!" No worry about keeping cool the beer and martinis alongside. If the fire under the hot water heaters died down, it was simply "more oil" to "give it a hot spark." No sense letting all that dirty, old motor oil go to waste.

I was surprised one hot afternoon after working with Dave on some "beater" of a car (Aunt Eleanor's?) when he offered me a *lawnmower* beer. *Lawnmower* beer? His strategy was simple and frugal. He said you don't much taste or appreciate your first beer in that thirsty situation, so you might as well drink the cheapest one available (like Brown Derby or Olympia). Follow it up with a fine imported Belgium beer to sip and enjoy. He then made the exhaling, relief sound of a horse shaking its head and letting some saliva fly, followed with an "Easy big fellah."

No one mimicked effeminate men like Dave. He liked to talk that way to truck drivers he could reach at night with his CB radio from his property, getting them all riled up. When he told us gay content jokes, he had us laughing through our tears when he gave the punch line to, for example, "The first coat's dry" and "Let the man rob the train the way he wants to." And he did.

Zucchini. He could never get enough of it. He must have dreamed of it the way young Navy men used to dream of you-know-what in Subic Bay, the Philippines (no, he dreamed of San Miguel when he was there and snuck some back aboard the ship). When I made him clam chowder, I put zucchini in it just for him. He called it a number "10." He rated some place at Bodega Bay a 9.5. Spenger's got a 9. When I camped with he and Tom at Smith Valley, Nevada, along with Denny and others, we ate nothing but zucchini, bean sprouts, tofu garden burgers, wheat bread, and a whole-grain cereal. My mouth salivated smelling Denny's and Jim Carey's steaks and John Ford's lobster cooking. I had to "shaken the bush, boss" 6 times a day with that stuff. Good thing Carey installed that seat over the sagebrush.

No one at Smith Valley in the 80's ever topped Dave's hot tub on wheels. He and Tom drove Denny, Jim, and others around the desert camp with a bathtub full of water sloshing around, set high in the rear of a VW dune buggy. Baths were taken in 1, agitating lap around the sage brush campsite while the bathees drank their favorite liquor (Denny liked one-half gallons of Crown Royal). The next day, Dave climbed 600 yards up a mountain nearby and set out a bowling ball he'd painted white just for us to have some target practice on. Everything from 2" .38 snubs to .22, .357, and .44 mag pistols to 30-06's and assorted police long arms rang out from the ragged firing line. Dave retrieved the ball the following day. The cops weren't very good marksmen.

Dave was meticulous with how he wanted things done. How he fixed and guaranteed the fixing of all those cars over all those years, how he painted his houses, how he hot-water mopped with TSP his garage floor 3 times/day, how he raked the gravel at his old campsite, how he "filleted" (16" exact), split, and stacked firewood, how he constructed the train site outside his house, how he built the bocce ball court, and in what order and how much he drank of his favorite beverages. His standards were high for himself, and he expected them of others, too.

Boy, he liked to run, anywhere, anytime, but especially scenic parks inhabited by "monkey women." He'd stop working on cars or some other job just to go on a "run date" with Tom, Jeff, Joe, even Janet. The San Ramon-Alamo ridge, the Dipsea, Armstrong Redwoods, even the "Bongo Straights" if he had to while at the firehouse. He ran so much he hurt his back, but he kept on running, running so fast the bounds couldn't catch him, down the Occidental to the Gulf Sebastopo.

Now the running is played out.

Oh, we're adults, we're supposed to know this is what happens.

But no, not to us, not to our "one for the road" Dave, not now.

He was supposed to be around a good long while, like his parents.

He prepared himself for that, and prepared us, too. No one really *likes* skim milk, but he drank it. Now, to our consternation, we won't have the consolation of one last "good mornin" from him while he's chewing some food and sipping a cup of Peet's, or one last "goodnight" with an E&J nightcap.

We're cheated, through no fault of his. Gone in a flash. That's the shock we feel.

And sadness about the expectations no more.

For what he'll miss of our continued lives, and we to miss of him without him.

Often the life of the party and in his own way, of our lives. That's the rub, our missing-to-be.

Bye Dave. It's a cliché, but we will miss you. That missing will go on until we are all missed.

We are also filled with sadness for your kids, Tom, Shelley, and Theresa, your brother Denny and sister Janet, all of their families, and your many other relatives. We wish them well.

Thank you.

CHAPTER 13

Listening

O ur culture puts a great deal of emphasis on speaking, which is a key reason for public speaking classes. Yet, if we as speakers aren't listened to we won't continue speaking very long.

For we as listeners, it is in the act of listening that we are provided with a great opportunity to learn about the world.

As Chapter 4 on *Audience Analysis* indicated, speakers need to be listener-centered in their speech preparation to increase their chance of being heard. If the speaker speaks to the concerns of the listener (and this is the speaker's responsibility), the listener is apt to listen.

During speech preparation, the speaker will need to listen to those he or she interviews. During the actual speech, the speaker will need to observe the audience's feedback about his or her speech and attempt to adjust to it.

Students in the class are an audience for the speaker, so everyone plays a supportive role most of the time. Considering that most speakers appreciate attentive listeners, classmates can portray a look of attention and interest on their face when listening to other's speeches.

This does not mean that listeners should uncritically accept whatever the speaker says. Public speaking centers on a single person conveying ideas in messages tailored for the audience. You as a listener need to critique how effective the speaker is in attempting to speak to you and the rest of the class so you can learn both from their techniques and from their content. If the speaker is being persuasive, you certainly need to think critically about the message to protect yourself from easily being swayed to a new idea or action.

Experience shows that people are not that skilled at listening. This is understandable given the multitude of ongoing stimuli competing for our attention and perception. Listeners do have many of their own legitimate concerns to think about when others presume to speak to them and hold their attention. Still, there is room for improved listening.

A. SUGGESTIONS FOR LISTENING TO A SPEECH

1. Think positive. Give the speaker the benefit of the doubt. Maybe you will hear something you had not previously thought of.

2. Sit comfortably in your seat and try to smile at the speaker. You will feel better and so will they. Common courtesy suggests that you make no distracting noises or movements.

3. Have an organizational sense in your mind of what the speaker is expected to say at different places in the speech. This will be much easier in the classroom setting where the instructor has established some speaking guidelines. When you hear these, take note of them, and if you do not remember them later, consider why something may have been omitted.

4. Attempt to determine the speaker's main idea and key supporting ideas, and if these fit the speech's intended purpose. Hear the speaker out to avoid prejudging their ideas.

5. Briefly evaluate the legitimacy of the speaker's evidence and reasoning as you hear them.

6. Overall, would you say the speaker was adequately prepared? Was the speech topic and content relevant to the audience?

7. Listen to the speaker's tone of voice and observe his or her gestures and facial expressions. Determine whether these fit the main idea and whether the speaker was sincere.

HOMEWORK #14

Provide a *yes* or *no* and give one concise reason *why* for each of the following:

1. Is there anything wrong with *not* listening to a boring speaker?

2. Can faking attention as a listener to a speaker be harmful?

CHAPTER 14

Persuasive Speeches

Persuasion is a common aspect of communication since people attempt to predict and control their environment. In the classroom setting, persuasion is the conscious verbal and nonverbal attempt by a speaker to bring about some desired action from an audience (normally, other students). You may want to convince your audience to vote for a certain candidate (check their name on the ballot), follow a certain food diet in their daily eating, avoid alcohol binge drinking, and so on. While it is common to speak about using persuasion to change someone's beliefs, attitudes, or point of view about some person or phenomenon, there is no way to confirm such changes without seeing the behavior that suggests such changes (and even that is not foolproof). While we would not expect it in classroom speeches, there are coercive regulations or laws combined with persuasive messages outside the classroom.

Self-centeredness in this application should not suggest a negative connotation since it is natural for people to seek to satisfy their individual desires. It is unlikely to be considered immoral if you attempt to persuade a family member to loan you $10 for gas or to give you a ride to school, or to convince an employer to hire you for a job (and so on).

While most students will not have to give formal persuasive speeches outside of the class, persuasive speeches are common during our daily everyday lives. Politicians give such speeches frequently. People in sales give such presentations to groups of people in an attempt to get the audience to buy their health care plan, their computer software package, their fleet of trucks, and so on. Persuasive speaking is an important part of a religious leader's activities. Attorneys deliver persuasive speeches to juries. Notice that even if you give no other formal persuasive speech in your life, you will frequently be on the receiving end of such communication. Knowing about how persuasion in speeches occurs can help you become a critical listener.

To persuade people, you have to provide them with an answer to a need of theirs, a justification to act. The listener has to be convinced that your belief, cause, person, or product will significantly improve his or her life. Otherwise they will have little reason to act. This requires you to be familiar with the audience's needs, desires, attitudes, knowledge, and previous behaviors, so you can refer to these in relation to the action you desire of the audience. With your audience analysis (including relevant motivation appeals), you can illuminate what you together have in common. This will increase the likelihood that listeners will identify with you and follow your prescribed action/s to satisfy something lacking (a need) in their lives. Your illumination of an audience need and a solution to satisfy that need will increase the audience's motivation to act. Your convincing listeners that you have a significant amount of similarities helps assure them that your specified action is the right thing to do.

People tend to change little by little, sometimes with sudden shifts and sometimes not at all. Simply hearing a speech rarely moves a person to act. Thus, think of planting a seed in the audience's mind that will be able to grow over the years. A strong attempt to change your listeners may easily backfire, as when parents attempt to force their son/daughter to stop being a friend with some other boy or girl. People who are authoritarian, dogmatic, or deeply committed to a cause tolerate little change. To persuade these latter people, you will have to institute a sustained campaign.

A. PLANNING STEPS

1. Clarify your persuasive goal: the specific action you desire of your audience
2. List the key characteristics of your listeners as revealed by your audience analysis (e.g., age, gender, values, etc.) that give insight to their potential motivation to act as you desire. Can you cite harms they can reasonably be expected to experience when their needs and desires are not satisfied?
3. Find enough legitimate evidence that can be discussed in the time allotted for the speech.
4. Verify your reasoning (by analogy, authority, cause-effect, generalization, etc.) is sound.
5. Create a solution and a plan of action that can reasonably be expected to resolve the difficulty.

B. ORGANIZATION OF THE PERSUASIVE SPEECH: THE MOTIVATED SEQUENCE[1]

1. *Attention step*: You have to initially say something in some appealing manner about the topic to be discussed so the audience will want to listen to you.

2. *Need Step*: You will have to describe how the audience is either currently suffering or will suffer in the future from some unsatisfied need or desire. Point out various ways the audience is being harmed.

3. *Satisfaction step*: Provide listeners with information (a solution) that shows how the harms can be minimized or overcome. Create a resolution statement here along with three main supporting reasons for following it.

4. *Visualization step*: Specify the benefits of incorporating the solution you propose as well as the negative (possibly ongoing) outcomes from not following the general idea in the Satisfaction step. Do not simply reiterate what has just been said in the Satisfaction Step but describe more specific, tangible outcomes. Explain how the solution resolves the harms.

5. *Action step*: Tell listeners exactly what behaviors to perform so they will be satisfied. Choose some simple, physical actions that are well within their capability and easy for them to do. Although you have created your speech in hope that the listeners will follow your actions, you may simply but importantly have moved the listeners one step closer to actually achieving the desired outcome.

See the Persuasive Speech outline at the end of this chapter for an illustration of these steps.

C. BUILD YOUR CREDIBILITY

To increase the likelihood that people will be persuaded, they have to, in part, believe in *you* as a person. For an audience to consider you credible, they evaluate what they perceive to be your character, intelligence, good will, and dynamism. Other terms for these factors are trustworthiness,/honesty, expertise, competence, sincerity or concern for others, and attractiveness, charisma, or personal energy. Remember, your credibility is in the eyes of the beholder—the audience.

The following are some methods for enhancing your credibility.[2]

1. *Character/honesty*: Refer to values, beliefs, and actions of yours that reveal common virtues, refer to memorable accomplishments revealing personal integrity but without boasting, use highly credible authorities to substantiate your claims, and discuss more than one side of any debatable points to increase your perceived fairness.

2. *Intelligence/competence/expertise*: Refer to your relevant experiences and successes. Show that your speech is well organized, and use valid evidence and reasoning to support your positions. Show that your recommendations follow generally accepted criteria; explain how they will solve the problems you've identified. Document your sources of information, and use a variety of sources. Use clear, simple visual aids when fitting, and deliver your speech in a calm and forthright manner.

3. *Good will/sincerity/friendliness*: Show personal warmth toward the audience by looking at them and speaking with both a friendly and sincere tone of voice. Give recognition to anyone who has helped you accomplish a relevant project. Refer to harms facing and/or experienced by your audience. Speak in a respectful manner despite possible differences of opinion; sound as if you are open to correction, and criticism should you be questioned.

4. *Dynamism/charisma/energy*: Speak vividly and create clear images. Use active rather than passive verbs, and concise wording as well as an animated body, direct eye contact, and upright posture. Dress appropriately for the occasion; and sound like you are enthused about the audience, the occasion, and the subject matter.

D. RESPONDING TO THE AUDIENCE'S GENERAL PREDISPOSITIONS[3]

An audience can have one of five general attitudes toward your topic and purpose.[4] Speakers can counteract these by using the responses accompanying each of the predispositions.

1. *Interested but undecided about what to do.* Explain to your audience the relevance of the subject to their lives, describe a few possible solutions, and then emphasize the one you think is most suitable for both you and them. Reinforce the benefits of your solution.

2. *Favorable but not aroused to act.* Verbally reinforce the audience's beliefs in the subject, then emphasize what is not being satisfied among it's primary needs. Describe the harms they are experiencing and/or face in the future and how certain specific actions will minimize or stop those harms.

3. *Interested in the situation but hostile to the proposed attitude, belief, value, or action.* Verbally confirm the good feelings listeners have about the topic then reiterate the harms they are receiving under the status quo. Enhance your own credibility by the methods noted earlier in this chapter. Appear fair in your discussion of different points of view of the topic. Effectively refute existing hostility by citing legitimate evidence and respected authorities. Follow this with a small range of possible solutions and use counter evidence to show that only one is a viable one.

4. *Apathetic toward the situation.* Recognize that you probably require multiple speech occasions to arouse apathetic listeners. Humor can help get their attention. Keep your message simple and direct. Clearly explain how the current situation and subject matter impinges upon their lives. Avoid being overbearing in your tone (do not sound "preachy").Visualize for them the tangible and realistic benefits they could receive by their specified involvement with the current situation.

5. *Hostile to any change from the present state of affairs.* This is a supreme challenge you face as a persuader. You are likely to get little, if any, hearing from such an audience. A third party may be needed to even force such people to attend your speech. They will have numerous counterarguments against your presumed position before you have begun speaking and may blame you for making them be there. In their minds they will be thinking that you cannot convince them. You will have to know of and have the ability to satisfy one key need in their lives, undoubtedly something outside the speech context. You cannot make the situation complicated since they have no motivation to process a range of factors.

Overall, justify to the listeners what is in their interest to do.

The use of humor can easily backfire if your listeners interpret it as manipulative or irrelevant to their lives (people who are on the defensive or upset about something don't interpret something said about a change as a joking matter).

Change

Your attempt to get the audience to change some aspect of their behavior may require you to reinforce a pre-existing condition. Refer (appeal) to "old" commitments, to the beliefs, values, knowledge, and/or attitudes already possessed by the audience members (Ehninger, 1986). For example, the audience may need to be reminded of the value of the group and its causes so that they will once more contribute their time, energy, and money to the tasks needed doing.

Recognize that changes in beliefs, values, or attitudes cannot be recognized apart from behaviors that seem to emulate them. Thus, your goal is not to simply change someone's belief about something but to use that mental change to instigate and bring about the behavior you are after. You can never be sure a cognitive change has occurred so you will have to infer this change based upon behavioral change you observe (if any).

Keep the speech short and direct. Initially speak to them where they are at—their position, then on future occasions target your message closer and closer to your position, describing the common ground you share with them. They have to perceive that there is an obvious benefit for aligning themselves with you. As with the above situations, use legitimate evidence and cite respected authorities.

CONCLUSION

Persuasion is an inherent aspect of our communication and in our lives as people negotiate their daily actions with each other. In speeches, there is a conscious attempt to encourage a certain action from the listeners. Speakers will typically be more successful if they attempt to get their listeners to take small steps in the direction of the ultimate goal. Make sure that these small steps are easily performed and within the listeners' capabilities.

E. SAMPLE PERSUASIVE SPEECH TOPICS: PROPOSITIONS AND SUPPORTING POINTS

1. Families should develop strong interpersonal bonds by maintaining common values, developing commitment with each other, and preserving cultural traditions.

2. Your should take proper care of your teeth to have a healthy smile, avoid general health problems, and to save money.

3. You should complain to oil companies (or the government) about high gas prices so prices at the pump are decreased, food prices are reduced, and people can drive their chose vehicle.

4. You should abstain from premarital sex to avoid unwanted pregnancies, sexually transmitted diseases, and divorce.

5. You must be a careful driver at night, on rainy days, and over long distances.

6. You should avoid smoking cigarettes since _____, _____, and _____.

7. Guam should become a commonwealth (or state, or independent nation) since/due to/because of _____, _____, and _____.

8. The police should arrest all traffic violators given _____, _____, and _____.

9. You should believe in the religious concept of creation since _____, _____, and _____.

10. You should not use illegal drugs since _____, _____, and _____.

11. You should eat healthily since _____, _____, and _____.

12. You should follow a regular workout program since _____, _____, and _____.

F. MOTIVATED SEQUENCE PERSUASIVE
SPEECH OUTLINE[6]

A. Introduction
  1. *Attention Step.* Do not mention problems/harms/suffering here, but describe a situation going well that relates to the topic. Be interesting.

  _____

  _____

  2. *Need/Problem Outcomes Step*: Here you have to show the audience that it lacks (has a need for something (such as: safety, physical health, financial security, happiness, career goals, power, etc.) by pointing out problem outcomes that negatively affect it (harms, suffering, such as: crime, death diabetes, job loss, lack of entertainment, high unemployment, increased school costs, injury, etc.). You want the audience to feel that something has to be learned or done due to something they are lacking or will negatively harm them. Follow these steps:
  a. Make a general statement about a harm (implying a need to be satisfied) that does or will exist for the audience (i.e., a statement about people suffering).

  _____

  _____

  b. Provide an illustration that reveals the problem outcomes/harms experienced by people.

  _____

  _____

  c. Provide ramifications of the need (the harms) that do or are likely to exist (additional illustrations, specific examples, statistics, testimony, definitions, visual aids) for your audience. Here on this form only list your data.

  _____

  _____

d. State clearly and directly to the class (audience) how these problem outcomes harm them. Be able to tell the audience that it is suffering or can be expected to suffer in the future.

B. Satisfaction Step: Body of the speech should last about 4 minutes in a 6 minute speech.

1. *Proposition*: Provide a grammatically complete sentence first, containing a persuasive word such as *should*. Then use connecting words like *since, due to, because, including*, etc., followed by three concise, main, supporting points that provide elaboration or justification for the proposition.

---

2. *Definitions of terms*: If there are key terms in the *thesis* only that require understanding. Do not define any supporting points here.

---

3. *Statement of first major point*. State it exactly as it is with the thesis above; *precede it* here with a transitional word/phrase.

Supporting information: Here on this form only list your data, and possibly define terms.

---

4. *Statement of second major point.* State it exactly as it is with the thesis above; *precede it* here with a transitional word/phrase.

_____

Supporting information: Here on this form only list your data, and possibly define terms.

_____

_____

5. *Statement of third major point.* State it exactly as it is with the thesis above; *precede it* here with a transitional word/phrase.

_____

Supporting information: Here on this form only list your data, and possibly define terms.

_____

_____

6. *Internal summary.* Restate the proposition with slightly different words having the same meaning and add the three supporting points stated *exactly* as they previously were.

_____

_____

C. *Visualization step*: Describe the consequences for doing what is asked for in the Satisfaction step. Do not merely repeat what has been previously said.

1. Benefits: _____

_____

2. Undesirable effects if not done: _____

_____

D.*Action step*: The specific action(s) you desire of the audience. Ask of them what is within their power, what is convenient and easy for them to accomplish.

_____

_____

References
1. _____.   2. _____.

G. SAMPLE PERSUASIVE SPEECH OUTLINE:
SAFETY GLASSES

A. Attention Step
1. I woke this morning to a sunlight-filled room, my eyes well rested, my vision clear. I gazed out the window at the blue sky over Pago Bay and the gentle aquamarine water moving rhythmically back and forth along the palm-tree lined shore. Another day in paradise.

B. Need Step
1. Still, not everyone can enjoy my experience for more than 2,000 Americans each day sustain an eye injury.[1]
2. When an air conditioning installation man drilled a hole through my cement wall and hit a steel bar, a piece of it floated into his left eye. When it would not wash out, he went to a clinic to have an eye surgeon pick the piece out of his eye with a needle, apply a few drops, then patch over his eye. He missed work the next day, costing him $120 in lost wages plus the $250 he paid the clinic.
3. According to OSHA, eye injuries in the workplace cost more than $300 million each year in medical costs, worker compensation, and production losses.[2] The University of Michigan Kellogg Eye Center reports that just over one-half of eye injuries each year occur to those under 25 and over 100,000 of these injuries are in sports or recreational pursuits.[3] People may lose their sight in one or both eyes, be unable to work at some jobs, be prevented from driving, cooking, and so on.
4. On Guam, like other places, most college students such as yourself work both at home and on paid jobs. You also enjoy sports and recreational activities, so you are at risk of suffering an eye injury.

C. Satisfaction Step
   1. You must wear safety glasses to protect your eyes, including on the job, at home, and in public.
   2. Safety glasses: specially constructed glasses that protect the eyes from the impact of flying objects.
   3. First, on the job.
      a. chemicals
      b. metal and wood splinters
      c. winging and falling objects.
   4. Second, at home.
      a. trimming grass and foliage
      b. house repairs
      c. vehicle repairs
   5. Third, in public.
      a. sports
      b. recreational activities
      c. motor vehicle traffic
   6. Internal Summary: It is essential that you use safety glasses on the job, at home, and in public.

D. Visualization Step
   1. Remember, the daily looks of love on the faces of your family and friends, who and what you saw at your surprise birthday party, your favorite ring or car, the perfect paint job you did on your sister's bedroom? The sunset out over the Philippine Sea as you dig your feet into the sand along Tumon Bay? The money you have to loan your brother from not having to spend it on medical bills and vision-impaired glasses? Can you even imagine the darkness that would descend unnecessarily over your world if your eyes were impaired? Now helpless and dependant, the record playing over and over in your mind about what you could have easily done differently that certain day?

E. Action Step
   1. Ask your employer to provide you with safety glasses, and wear them. Buy them, if necessary.
   2. Buy your family safety glasses for $10 each at any hardware store. Insist that everyone wear them when doing any project. Lead by example. Put extra pairs in your car for when you're out in public. The next time you're overlooking the bay, any bay, consider the beauty of what you see.

SPEECH REFERENCES

1. "Eye injury prevention month," *Federal Occupational Health*, U.S. Dept. of Health, 2011.
2. "Eye and face protection," *OSHA*, http://www.osha.gov/SLTC/eyeface protection/index.html.
3. "Eye injuries," University of Michigan Kellogg Eye Center, http:/www.kellogg.umich.edu/patientcare/conditions/eye.injuries.html

REFERENCES

1. Ehninger, D., Gronbeck, B., McKerrow, R., and Monroe, A. *Principles and Types of Speech Communication*, 10th ed. Glenview, IL: Scott, Foresman and Company, 1986.
2. Ibid.
3. Ibid.
4. Ibid.
5. Ibid.
6. Ibid.

HOMEWORK #15

Provide a 15-20 item questionnaire about your persuasive speech topic that the class will fill out before your speech. Create questions that will help you discover the knowledge, beliefs, values, attitudes, and behaviors of theirs' that are related to your topic and what actions you can expect of them. Questions should solicit brief responses. Make sufficient copies for the entire class.

Sample Questionnaire: Legal Alcohol Drinking Age.

Directions: circle or fill in the appropriate answer.

1. Your age:____
2. Male or Female
3. In the military (active/reserves/national guard)? Yes No
4. Do you drink alcoholic beverages: Yes No
5. How old were you when you first drank an alcoholic beverage? ____
   Never ____

6. If you drink alcohol, how often do you drink?

   Daily   3-4 times/week   1/week   1-2/month   Special occasions only.

7. If you previously drank alcohol but stopped, explain why:_____
8. Do your parents drink alcoholic beverages? Yes No
9. If your parents previously drank but stopped, explain why: ____
10. Do you have children: Yes No (if no, go directly to question #12)
11. Do you provide a good role model of safe/responsible drinking for your children? Yes No
12. Are you registered to vote? Yes No
13. If registered, do you vote? Yes No
14. Do you know how many people on Guam died of alcohol-related diseases last year? Yes No
15. The age 18-20 group, when allowed to publicly drink on Guam, had a significant number of DUIs and/or traffic accidents over the years:

    Strongly disagree   Slightly disagree   Don't know   Slightly agree   Strongly agree

16. Lowering the legal drinking age to 18 will significantly curtail under-21 binge drinking:

    Strongly disagree   Slightly disagree   Don't know   Slightly agree   Strongly agree

17. Lowering the legal drinking age to 18 will significantly increase under-21 sexual activity:

    Strongly disagree   Slightly disagree   Don't know   Slightly agree   Strongly agree

18. Lowering the legal drinking age to 18 will significantly increase under-21 physical violence, including rape:

    Strongly disagree   Slightly disagree   Don't know   Slightly agree   Strongly agree

19. Drinking alcohol is simply bad for our body, or a sin, or both:

    Strongly disagree   Slightly disagree   Don't know   Slightly agree   Strongly agree

20. If you can legally vote on this issue, will you vote to lower the legal drinking age to 18?

    Strongly disagree   Slightly disagree   Don't know   Slightly agree   Strongly agree

HOMEWORK #16

One week in advance of your Persuasive Speech, submit an outline of it using the form provided a few pages earlier in this chapter.

Speaking Assignments, Sample Speeches, Evaluations Forms

MEMORABLE MOMENT

This 2-3 minute speech focuses on one event, be it exciting, embarrassing, scary, or other. You have told your friends and family members many stories about your experiences. Now tell one of these to us. We cannot expect you to know much about speech making at this point in the class, but you should be able to do the following.

Guidelines

1. Choose an event that you well remember and could easily talk about right now.

2. At home, consider writing down the time order of events to verify your details are in order. Be descriptive of what occurred rather than simply say "It was fun/exciting/boring/etc." By how you describe the event, we should know if it was fun, scary, embarrassing, or whatever. Verbally go over the details to verify the content, order, and length

3. Begin the speech with the first detail of the story (e.g., "One day when I was 7, my cousin and I ...."), then continue on with the details of the story so we can imagine being there. Do not begin the speech with: "This is about the most memorable/scary/etc. moment in my life."

4. Be succinct with the content of the story, telling us just what we need to know without the unnecessary details. Of course the story has to be at least 2 minutes long. Do not add unnecessary details to meet the minimum time. If one story is too long, choose another one.

5. Practice at home speaking in complete phrases or sentences. Avoid pausing where there would be no comma or period (e.g., "When I was ... 7, my cousin ... and I ...went for a hike. If you errantly pause, avoid filler words or sounds such as: uh, um, like, you know, etc.

6. With your voice, make some changes in loudness, rate, pitch, pauses, and tone of voice to help convey the meaning and feeling of the story. You already do this when you tell stories to others as a way to create a mental picture of what has occurred. For example, when people are excited they speak faster, when scared they often use a higher pitch and give a shaking sound to their voice, when bored they speak slowly with a monotone and lower pitch, and so on.

7. Do not give away in advance a surprise that may come up later in the story.

8. In your concluding sentence (or two), use your voice to combine with your words to let us know that you are about to finish. People usually speak slower and with a lower pitch. After your final word, avoid saying "The end," "Thank you," "The moral to of the story is ....," or "That was the most exciting ..." We should already know this by your speech.

9. Brief notes or an outline can be used. A complete written out account of the story is not allowed. This speech is about one event that you've probably already told to someone else, so a written account is not needed. We want you to be able to speak to us, not to your notes.

Evaluation: time (2-3 minutes), loudness + vocal changes, organization, succinctness, phrasing, use or not of filler words/sounds, and conclusion (what and how it is said).

MEMORABLE MOMENT SPEECH[1]

It was on December 12th, 1999, and I was ready to run the Honolulu Marathon.

Before the 5:00 AM cannon blast to start the race, I was with 8 runners from Guam and about 30,000 others from all over the world. We saw the most beautiful 5 minute fireworks display that shot over Ala Moana Beach Park opposite the well-known shopping center.

My friend, Mary, cheered me on as I waited to start. "Go, Madeline!" The rain poured on us while we waited 10 minutes to begin moving after the runners in front first took off. There were so many people around us.

As I began my run, I told myself to stay relaxed, not to increase my speed, and drink a lot of water to prevent "hitting the wall."

The 5-mile point was Kapiolani Park at the lower end of Waikiki, right before the run up and around Diamond Head Crater. Even though I felt strong, relaxed, and very prepared for this race, my nerves got the best of me and brought on the urgency to find a pit stop. I didn't see any portable johns but I did find a small bush and that was all I needed.

By this time, the Guam group was about 5 miles ahead of me so I was on my own. I remember saying a prayer and asking our Lord to stay close to me because I felt lost among the 30,000 people. I managed to bring my stress level down and I had a consistent, strong run all the way up the Diamond Head pass and over to Highway 1. While on H-1, I heard a voice. "Hey Maddy, is that you? Slow down so we can run with you." It was unbelievable. My adrenaline and prayer had spurred me on to reunite me with my group. What are the chances of that happening?

My friend and I were running side-by-side through Hawaii Kai and down to Kahala Ave. On and on we went, one grueling step after another, as the route led to Hawaii Kai and circled back to Kahala Ave and Diamond Head Road toward Waikiki. At the 26-mile point we were both exhausted but at the Kapiolani Park finish line we held our hands in the air together as we completed the race! I had been able to finish in the top 10% of my age group with a race time of 4:49:56.

After the event, I had to show Mary the bush in the park I had used as my pit stop early in the race. I looked all over for it but could not find it next to the race route. There was no bush where I had stopped. Did I moon thousands of people at 5:30 AM?

SAMPLE MEMORABLE MOMENT
SPEECH EVALUATION FORM

_____ Memorable Moment Speech

_____	
(name)	Time (2-3 minutes)
Organized: from the beginning to the end Introduction: avoided mentioning type of story	0 1 2 3 4
Delivery: loud enough, varied voice to convey emotions	0 1 2 3 4
Phrasing: words grouped into thought units, phrases, or sentences — given the content. Choppy?	0 1 2 3 4
Inarticulate/filler words (um/uh/and/you know/ok/ etc.)	0 1 2 3 4
Eye contact: from the beginning to the end	0 1 2 3 4
Succinct: told as briefly as possible, given the event Too long? Too short?	0 1 2 3 4
Conclusion: rate & duration appropriate to the ending, Tone of voice fitting, avoided "moral of story"	0 1 2 3 4
Amount grade lowered due to excessive shortness or length?	

[0-inadequate, 1-adequate, 2-good, 3-very good, 4-excellent] Grade _____

CRITICISM SPEECH

This is a 2-3 minute speech that is to familiarize yourself with the Need Step in the Motivated Sequence organizational form.[2] It is labeled a _criticism_ speech since it's purpose is to critique a harmful situation experienced or expected to be experienced by the audience. The Need Step, which is being used here as a complete speech, is supposed to create a desire in your listeners to listen to your Satisfaction Step—your solution to the problem situation facing the audience. As previously explained in Chapter 6, a *need* is a perceived lack of something that the individual wants satisfied or fulfilled. The Need Step also provides justification for the speaker's thesis.

The speaker has to create a sense of urgency about an existing condition that will make the listeners receptive to some satisfying information (or even action to resolve the situation, as in a persuasive speech). Speaking to the audience needs increases the speaker's credibility since the speaker shows that he or she is in touch with a troubling situation affecting the listeners. Elaborate on the suffering caused by some condition or phenomenon (crime, poor diet, no monetary savings, etc.), which will show the audience that it lacks (has a need for) something (such as: safety, physical health, financial security, happiness, career goals, etc.). You want the audience to feel that something has to be learned or done to resolve the problematic situation.

Imagine yourself having bad experiences with cars, restaurants, government agencies, product packaging, hospital care, being broke, and so on. Or, explain how some law is harming us or how people are suffering under the enforcement of some law. What are the everyday foibles of our lives that harm us?

The Criticism Speech should incorporate the sub-steps of the Need Step, as follows:

1. Make a general statement about the existence of some harm (some suffering), implying that the audience has this need to be satisfied or resolved. Avoid causes and/or solutions.
2. Provide an illustration (concise detailed story) that reveals the existing problem outcomes (harms, suffering) being experienced by a specific person. Avoid causes and/or solutions.
3. Provide ramifications of the problem outcomes/harms/suffering—that do or are likely to exist (additional illustrations, specific examples, statistics, testimony, definitions, visual aids) for your audience. Avoid causes and/or solutions.
4. State clearly to the audience (the class) that they are or will suffer these problem outcomes. Avoid causes and/or solutions.

Remember, it is in the Need Step that you connect your subject to the important interests of your audience. Audience analysis of the audience is necessary to complete this step.

Outline of Criticism Speech

1. Begin your speech with a one-sentence introduction to the problem topic area.
2. Develop, in the order listed above, each of the 4 parts of the Need Step, describing something you find harmful (referencing the suffering in each step).
3. End your speech with a one or two sentence conclusion summarizing the harm. You may offer a one sentence general remedy or solution for the suffering, but do not elaborate on this.

Other examples of phenomenon that may be critiqued: the customer service at public agencies or private businesses; poor student health care, financial aid, advising, text book costs, etc. at University of ___; war/war in Iraq or elsewhere; physical abuse; the high cost of living on Guam or elsewhere, litter; poor nutritional diet/fiesta diet; poor roads on Guam; dirty public bathrooms; low individual/family financial savings rate, excessive consumerism, cigarette smoking, and so on.

SAMPLE CRITICISM SPEECH: *DIABETES*[3]

1. Before 1944, the people of Guam were slender, subsisting on a diet of fish, vegetables, fruit, and grain, often cooked with coconut oil.

2. a. Today, this has largely changed. A significant number of people on Guam are overweight and unnecessarily suffering from diabetes. According to Guam Seventh Day Adventist physician Dr. Wes Youngberg, "Adult on-set diabetes, often referred to as Type II diabetes, is common in Polynesia and Micronesia, typically occurring in adults age 40 and above. The prevalence of diabetes on Guam is quite high."

   b. Mr. Castro lived a typical life on Guam, enjoying the many fiestas and the local food. When he was 36 he weighed 280 pounds and was diagnosed with Type 2 diabetes, which often leads to the #1 cause of death on Guam — heart disease. Mr. Castro constantly felt fatigued so he did no chores around his house. He could not play any sports with his boys, who became his errand boys. Intimacy with his wife was greatly diminished, who also blamed herself for much of the unhealthy food he ate. He took excessive days off work which led him to lose $200/ month (his wife has no income). Extra doctor visits cost him $100/ month in additional co-payments. At this rate, he could, unfortunately, look forward to an early demise, leaving his wife and kids destitute.

c. On November 13, 2006, a Pacific Daily News article estimated that 60% of Chamorro (20,000+) on Guam have either Type 2 diabetes or the pre-diabetic condition termed impaired glucose tolerance. 5% of diabetics will have a foot amputated, 5% will go blind, and 10% will have kidney failure by 60 and die. The cost to have one foot amputated was about $2,640 and the healing takes months. Lost eyesight inevitably leads to a lost job and the approximate annual income of $25,000. Kidney treatment requires 3 visits/week to the Dialysis Center, and without insurance costs $600/ visit, $1800/week, $7,200/month, and $86,400/year. At the end, funerals cost $6,000 plus. Many on Guam are dying at an early age, between 45-65, due to diabetes, for life expectancy is reduced between 20-30 years. Children as young as 12 have been diagnosed with Type 2 diabetes on Guam, and with so many obese kids on Guam this will increase the likelihood that they will have diabetes as adults.

d. Many people on Guam have a poor diet and limited exercise so your friends and fellow students are likely to develop diabetes. For every person in your family who you know has diabetes, there is at least one other who has it but does not know it yet. According to Dr. Youngberg, "You might have diabetes since it can be genetically inherited and so many people on Guam have it." Thus, the lifestyle and genes on Guam endanger many of us.

3. This is not pleasant information, but if you are an overweight Chamorro or Filipino, live a sedentary life, and have a family history of diabetes, the information suggests that you probably already have Type 2. It is recommended that all people over 45 be tested and seek immediate medical help.

CRITICISM SPEECH EVALUATION FORM

_____ Criticism Speech

_____
(name)   Time (2-3 minutes)

Introduction: General statement of a problem situation (some group of people suffering); Loud clear voice.	0 1 2 3 4
Illustration of someone experiencing the harms of the problem situation (a concise description of the suffering).	0 1 2 3 4
Ramifications: Additional examples, illustrations, testimony, data, and other support showing the extent of the suffering.	0 1 2 3 4
Pointing: Concise, convincing explanation of how the harms (the suffering) are or will be experienced by the audience.	0 1 2 3 4
Eye contact: Continual, appropriate use of notes.	0 1 2 3 4
Delivery: Phrasing, filler words, loudness, sincere voice tone.	0 1 2 3 4
Amount grade lowered due to excessive shortness or length?	

[0-inadequate, 1-adequate, 2-good, 3-very good, 4-excellent] Grade _____

SPEECH OF INTRODUCTION

[Two weeks before this speech is to be delivered, submit a 1-2 page biography of yourself (accurate, fantasy, or mixed), to be given by your teacher to another classmate who will use it to prepare a speech to introduce you. They will be free to use all, part, or even none of what you submit. You will be given someone else's biography and create a speech to introduce them]

This is a 2-3 minute speech in which you will introduce a classmate. This type of speech is given immediately before a featured speaker presents his or her own speech in an attempt to create in the audience a favorable image of both the featured speaker and his or her message. This introduction is normally delivered by a member of the group that has arranged for the speech occasion. To be effective, the introduction speech needs to stimulate a desire in the audience to want to hear the featured speaker. Inform or remind the audience of the speaker's position in the community or within the organization and his or her accomplishments. [Your role is neither to make the expected speech or air your own views on the subject to be discussed by the main speaker nor call undue attention to yourself.] You are only the speaker's advance agent and your job is to sell him or her to the audience.

Speeches of introduction are supposed to help create a friendly relationship between the speaker and the audience. They are to dispel potential fear about the unknown person (if that is the case) and/or their topic, and they should bring about a closeness between the speaker and the audience. If the main speaker's expertise is known, as well, then the speech of introduction can be expected to raise the credibility of the featured speaker.

A. TWO GOALS/RESPONSIBILITIES

1. Arouse the listener's curiosity about the speaker and/or subject.
2. Generate audience respect for the speaker to help his or her message acceptance.

B. PREPARATION STEPS

Create a speech of introduction for the person you've been given a biography. You can accept all or part or none of what they say about themselves. You will have to create a verbal context, a scenario in which you will be introducing this person. For example, you might introduce them as a medical doctor to speak on topic of medicine, a professional athlete to discuss dedication, a philanthropist to discuss benefits of charities, etc.

1. Purpose and manner of speaking
   Know your function. You are providing a service, which is to create for the speaker a position of prominence. You do not want to draw undue attention to yourself.

2. Formulating the content
Learn about the speaker, his or her background and biographical data. Arrange a personal interview, if necessary. Be certain all your information is accurate. Know how to correctly pronounce his or her name.

    a. Be brief. As a general rule, saying too much is worse than saying nothing at all. Two to three minutes in length should be sufficient.

    b. Talk about the speaker. Who are they? What is their position in education, business, the community, etc.? Summarize the speaker's primary qualifications to speak on the announced subject but don't overdo it to the point of embarrassment. "Don't bore your audience with a long recital of the speaker's biography or with a series of anecdotes about your acquaintance with the person."[4] You can use humor but ensure it is in good taste.

    c. Emphasize the importance of the speaker's subject and describe how it is relevant to the audience's interests. Only make general comments about the speaker's topic area. Do not praise or blame the speaker's ability as a speaker. Let the speaker emphasize his or her own knowledge and skills.

C. ORGANIZING THE SPEECH:

1. Use a brief opening to get the audience's attention and interest.
2. Develop 2-3 main points of interest about the speaker.
3. Finish with a key statement about the person and a reference to his or her topic.

For the final statement of your speech, you should make a statement to let the speaker know that the time to speak has come. For example, you might say, "Now to speak to us about _____, Mr./Ms._____" or "Let's give a warm welcome to Mr./Ms._____" After this conclusion, turn toward the speaker and lead the audience's applause.

SAMPLE SPEECH OF INTRODUCTION[5]

Good afternoon graduates, family members, friends, faculty, Board of Regents, and distinguished guests.

Many University of Guam students select majors that will help fulfill their career goals and their financial dreams. It was 20 years ago when a University of Guam Communication major said in an informative speech that, "the cure for diabetes should be vital to you." His listeners knew it to be true since so many on Guam and in Micronesia suffered from it, but what was the answer? Fortunately, that answer was vital to that speaker.

After graduating from the University of Guam, this person attended Loma Linda Medical Center for Preventive Medicine in Southern California where he began a 20 year journey around the world teaching and researching preventive medicine. We know that doctors don't get rich working for SDA and that isn't their goal, anyway. We also know that medical facilities and living conditions can be deplorable in many parts of the world, but that's where the people and diseases largely exist. This doctor wasn't doing his research in the Mayo Clinic. Following many setbacks and the constant budget constraints we all recognize, and with the continual mentoring of Dr. Wes Youngberg, he made a breakthrough in his quest for a diabetes cure. For this he was awarded the 2025 Nobel Prize in physics and given a $1.5 million religion award by the Seventh Day Adventists.

When asked in Sweden how he did it, he replied, "Many people don't realize that science basically involves assumptions and faith. Wonderful things in both science and religion come from our efforts based on careful observations, thoughtful assumptions, logic, and faith." He cited his 2010 discovery of Master Principles as an example. While sitting on a park bench reading the Bible verse in the book of Matthew 21, verse 22, it states: "All things, whatsoever ye shall ask in prayer, believing, ye shall receive." This guided his behavior as he concentrated his efforts toward synthesizing what became the Principles.

We are very fortunate to have our University of Guam alumnus deliver the Commencement Address at this Spring, 2026 graduation ceremony. Anchored in his faith in a largely secular world, with perseverance to help change for the better the lives of millions and even billions of people, he will describe the journey that made his dream come true, just as it can for our current students. This will help our UOG students see how they, too, can achieve their goals after leaving this campus.

Members of the University of Guam family and community, someone who will share how the Bible sparked his dream for success, speaking on the topic, *Follow Your Dreams*, I am honored to present Dr. Hawley Iseke, Jr. [turn toward the side—this imaginary person—and clap moderately enthusiastically]

SPEECH OF INTRODUCTION EVALUATION FORM

_____ Speech of Introduction

_____
(name)   Time (2-3 minutes)

Opening statement: gain attention/interest, eye contact, loud clear voice, welcome speaker	0 1 2 3 4
Development of the person's background: expertise, knowledge, skills, experience (not embarrassing extent)	0 1 2 3 4
Importance and/or appropriateness of the person and the subject of the speech they'll give	0 1 2 3 4
Organization of the information	0 1 2 3 4
Conclusion: reference to what the person will immediately speak about; increasingly firm voice with a sense of expectancy/excitement	0 1 2 3 4
Anticipation created for the introduced person	0 1 2 3 4
Eye contact	0 1 2 3 4
Phrasing: fluid or choppy; filler words/sounds	0 1 2 3 4
Delivery: loudness, rate, word emphasis, sincerity	0 1 2 3 4
Style: words chosen to convey ideas & feelings	0 1 2 3 4
Conciseness; length (2-3.5 minutes) fit (or) not	

[0-inadequate, 1-adequate, 2-good, 3-very good, 4-excellent] Grade _____

INFORMATIVE SPEECH

This is a 6-8 minute speech in which you are to inform your audience about some topic. The speech should provide greater depth and breadth of understanding on a subject. About three-fourths of what you say should be new information or provide a new point of view to the majority of your listeners.

An outline *on the form provided* (*only*) is due one week before the speech to allow time for it to be critiqued and returned for possible revisions. A final copy of the outline is due when you deliver the speech. This copy will receive a homework grade

Motivated Sequence for the Informative Speech: see Chapter 10 for the form to use.

SAMPLE INFORMATIVE SPEECH: *NEWSTART*[6]

A. Introduction

1. *Attention Step*. Many people "ooo" and "ahh" over good-looking people at the top of their game. On Guam, the pro jet skier Topher Barretto and the pro racecar driver Romeo Barcenilla look ideally healthy. My, what did *they* have for breakfast?

2. *Need Step*:

   a. Yet, too many people assume that the slender, active, attractive teenagers and young adults we meet are healthy. We don't even stop to think about it.

   b. Gene Cruz, a very fit 35-year-old, was unaware of his high blood sugar level. At 45, he had one foot amputated, at 55 he went blind, and at 60 he died of kidney failure. His wife will get one-half of his Gov't of Guam retirement check but it is already difficult to get by on a full check so she'll be dependent on retired family members to add to that, leaving them stressed about paying their own bills. Worse yet, Gene's wife mourns for him daily.

   c. The reality is that 50% of the people on Guam suffer from having high blood sugar, at levels from 225-300 ppm. An individual within this range can expect to be diagnosed with diabetes and have its physical and financial costs. According Guam's Seventh Day Adventist (SDA) Wellness Center, 5% of diabetics will have a foot amputated, 5% will go blind, 10% will have kidney function failure, and they may have a heart attack.

Cost (in dollars)	Per Day	Weekly	Monthly	Yearly
Blood sugar meter				80
Strips	3	21	90	1080
Insulin Medication	3.57	25	107	1303
Total				2463
Dialysis Center	600	1800	7812	93,744
Foot amputated				2,640
Total				96,384

d. You, too, may contract diabetes, given the frequent genetic transmission on Guam, the poor diet prevalent here, and the lack of exercise common amongst students. If you're fortunate enough not to get it, one of your family members probably will.

B. Satisfaction Step (body)
1. *Thesis*: NEWSTART reverses diabetes by decreasing total fats, increasing dietary fiber, and instituting a regular exercise routine.
2. *Definition of terms*:
    a. NEWSTART: an acronym that stands for Nutrition (whole plant-based foods), Exercise (45-60 minutes/day of aerobics), Water (6-8 cups of pure water/day), Sunshine (regular early morning or late afternoon, neither intensity nor burning), Temperance (avoid harmful substances and use in moderation good things), Air (regular outdoor recreation with diaphragm breathing or oxygenation of blood), Rest (regular sleeping and balancing work with relaxation), and Trust (trust in God).
3. First, NEWSTART decreases total fats. High fats such as meat, vegetable oils, fried foods, and excessive sugar are physically unhealthy. Fat consumption raises blood sugar level, which causes diabetes. With NEWSTART, the individual is taken off these products. No more steak, spare ribs, fried chicken, Spam, chorizo, or Big Macs. No more red or white rice, Winchell's or Crown donuts, Chamorro punch, beer, Bacardi, burgundy wine, and the like. Given the cultural identification with and tastes of these foods and drinks, we can recognize the challenge of excluding these sources of fat from our diet. Many of the common meats eaten have 5-20 grams of fat at 9 calories per gram. Thus, someone could be getting 20 g. X 9 c. = 180 calories from fat high in trans fats, as well—all from what amounts to 1 ounce of steak. This is a lot of calories.

   NEWSTART, with its omission of such sources of fat from our diet, lowers fat to less than 10 grams/day. This in turn decreases insulin resistance and decreases total calories. Whole grains (whole wheat, bran) can be used as a meat substitute. For example, a veggie burger is low in fat. Whole grains plus beans compliment each other as a meat/protein substitute.
   [other information included here]

4. Second, NEWSTART increases dietary fiber to decrease insulin resistance. Caloric dense foods are processed foods such as white flour, sugar, and fats, which are found in all fast food restaurants, among other places. These are low in dietary fiber.
   [other information included here]

When increasing dietary fiber, people are eating nutrient dense food rather than caloric dense food. Increasing dietary fiber lowers blood sugar. NEWSTART promotes nutrient dense foods, which are plant based whole food. These include fresh broccoli, bok choy, and other green leafy vegetables; whole grains such as brown rice, whole-wheat flour, oat bran, all types of beans, nuts, and fresh fruit—especially blue berries. Green vegetables such as green beans and colored vegetables such as purple cabbage are other dense foots providing dietary fiber. Dietary fiber slows the absorption of glucose into the cells, adds to the bulk of the food eaten, and lowers cholesterol. In addition to decreasing blood sugar, people will lose weight and reduce risk of complications. .

5. Lastly, instituting a regular exercise routine is another NEWSTART change. It is apparent that many Americans do not exercise enough, given the high number of overweight Americans and the extraordinary incidences of both heart attacks, and diabetes (although these are not just exercise related).
[other information included here, omitted for brevity sake]

When exercising, peoples' muscles burn sugar for energy that reduces blood sugar. NEWSTART gets its clients to actively exercise 45-60 minutes/day so they will burn fat and calories. Simply walking will allow a person to burn up 360-500 calories. This will lower their insulin level that will make their body's cells sensitive to recognizing insulin, and they will loose weight. This will reduce the risk factors and people will feel healthy.
[other information included here, omitted for brevity sake]

C. Conclusion
1. Summary. Diabetes can be turned back and its symptoms minimized from following NEWSTART which decreases total fats, increases dietary fiber, and instituting a regular exercise routine. People following this will burn more fat, incur a lower insulin level, and physically feel much better.

2. Further thought. NEWSTART is not just a diet and exercise routine but a lifestyle change to create a longer, healthier life. This program takes a natural approach to bringing about health and decreases the need for medications or surgery. It also offers a method for preventing those with pre-diabetes from actually getting diabetes.

REFERENCE

Guam Seventh Day Adventist Wellness Center, April, 2005.

INFORMATIVE SPEECH EVALUATION FORM

_____ Informative Speech Evaluation

(name)	Time (6-8 minutes)

Intro. Attn. Step (gained attention, topic reference, credibility)	0 1 2 3 4
Need Step (statement, illustration, ramifications, pointing) a. b. c. d.	0 1 2 3 4
Thesis (clear, appropriate, w/3 supporting points)	0 1 2 3 4
Body (main points coherent, organized, unified) Definitions 1. 2. 3.	0 1 2 3 4
Development/support: specific, relevant, sufficient valid reasoning 1. 2. 3.	0 1 2 3 4
Transitions used, and at key places between main points:	0 1 2 3 4
Conclusion: 1. Thesis reference, summary main points 2. Further thought 3. voice—sense of finality	0 1 2 3 4
Visual aid: helpful purpose, used effectively	0 1 2 3 4
Subject selection: suits audience/occasion	0 1 2 3 4
Eye contact and appropriate use of notes	0 1 2 3 4
Delivery: phrasing, loudness, rate, pronunciation	0 1 2 3 4
Fit time limit (6-8 minutes) or not?	0 1 2 3 4

[0-inadequate, 1-adequate, 2-good, 3-very good, 4-excellent] Grade _____

SPECIAL OCCASION SPEECH:
GOOD WILL, COURTESY, ENTERTAINING

This is a 2.5-5 minute speech in which you will stress the significance of a person, group, idea, phenomenon, goal, event, place, or action (or some combination of these). In so doing, the identity and value of that being accentuated is celebrated and reinforced among the audience (Osborn & Osborn, 1991). The speech should encourage the members to be more appreciative of what they have in common and even what they may become in the future.

Types of Special Occasion (ceremonial) Speeches

There are a variety of ceremonial speeches, including: Speeches of Good Will, Courtesy (Welcoming, Acceptances, & Toasts), Entertaining/After Dinner, and Introduction.

Good Will speeches include, but are not limited to, farewells, wedding anniversaries, funerals, fund-raising campaign kickoffs and celebrations, beginning or end of the year events, political rallies, awards banquets, and other celebrations. According to Ehninger (1986), this speech should increase the listener's appreciation of a person, product, service, or procedure.

SAMPLE SPECIAL OCCASION SPEECH:
GOOD WILL (*CEREMONY*)[7]

Thank you, Mr. Iseke, and you in the audience for that warm welcome of introduction. I would also like to thank you for this beautiful medal of accomplishment.

I am very excited to accept this special medal for finishing in the top 10% of women at the master's level in the Honolulu Marathon.

I have been a member of the Guam Runner's Club—your club—since 1998. We have 500 dedicated runners who come out rain or shine. For some of us, running provides a time to relieve stress from work; for others, to socialize; for still others, to primarily enjoy being outdoors. It's amazing to think that we can even become addicted to sweating, as if we don't already get enough of it in our daily lives. I am delighted to say that while we all run for varied reasons, we have one overall goal and that is to stay healthy. One specific running goal I had for this last year was to enter and finish a marathon before I turned the age of 50 years young. I am happy to have finally done that.

During my 8 months of training for the marathon, my trials were many. They began with waking up at 4:45 to meet friends three times a week for a

5 AM fun run. Oh, the days I craved to just turn over and go back to sleep in that warm soft bed. Still, with great difficulty, I was able to ease toward the edge of the bed and then onto the floor. When I fell into the holes and tripped on the deep cement cracks of Guam's streets and sidewalks, I became discouraged. Upon running up Nimitz Hill, I would think, "Why am I doing this?" There were some moments of success when my body felt strong enough to run 10-18 miles and call them an easy run.

I am not the star today, for every runner in this room who accomplishes a goal should be recognized. You are setting a good example for people of all age categories that health is the answer to living a happier life.

I would like to recognize Dr. Youngberg who was my personal preventive care specialist.

He diligently researched supplements that would enhance my endurance and recommended proper food nutrients for energy that would keep me healthy while running 35-40 miles a week.

He repeatedly encouraged me to stick with it. If all runners can support at least one new person in taking up the sport, we would create a positive image for our community and help an ever-widening group of people with their health.

Guam's Runner's club was gracious to acknowledge me as the oldest woman to finish the marathon. I share this medal with each one of you, especially those who have striven for a dream.

Thank you very much.

SPECIAL OCCASION SPEECH EVALUATION FORM

_____ Special Occasion Speech Evaluation

_____

(name)   Time (2.5-5 minutes)

Introduction (gained attention, subject clear)	0 1 2 3 4
Body: _magnification_ of event/service/person/group; interesting facts; magnification built toward conclusion [if entertaining speech, support materials entertaining]	0 1 2 3 4
Identification (bond created, w/stories, heroes, renewal)	0 1 2 3 4
Conclusion (reference to theme, finality-voice)	0 1 2 3 4
Common theme throughout	0 1 2 3 4
Good Will speech enhanced audience's appreciation of a specific phenomenon	0 1 2 3 4
Entertaining speech (humor tasteful)	0 1 2 3 4
Language clear, concrete, vivid	0 1 2 3 4
Eye contact & appropriate use of notes	0 1 2 3 4
Delivery: voice used expressively, phrasing	0 1 2 3 4
Fit time limit (2.5-5 minutes) or not?	

[0-inadequate, 1-adequate, 2-good, 3-very good, 4-excellent] Grade_____

PERSUASIVE SPEECH

This is a 6-8 minute speech in which you will attempt to alter some set of beliefs, values, and/or attitudes that may reasonably be expected to lead to some audience change of behavior.

An outline _on the form provided_ (_only_) in Chapter 14 is due one week before the speech to allow time for it to critiqued and returned for possible revisions. A final copy of the outline is due when you deliver the speech, receiving the homework grade. Only a detailed outline will be permitted during the speech, no complete manuscripts. Being extemporaneous will help you with your persuasion. Be sure to use your audience analysis findings gained from the questionnaire you had the class fill out. Review the audience's knowledge of the topic, their general predisposition toward it, their reference groups (if any), that audience's thinking ability to understand what you're saying, and how credible your orientation toward the topic is likely to seem to them.

SAMPLE PERSUASIVE SPEECH:
OKINAWAN HEALTH PLAN[8]

A. Introduction
   1. *Attention Step*: It's nice to be able to walk along the beach when the mood strikes you, do a little snorkeling, play a little beach volleyball, or participate in a 1-on-1 or 2-on-2 basketball game at the community center. Some of you have no doubt hiked to Sigua Falls or up Mt. Lam Lam. Yet not everyone can do these activities, if they were so inclined.

   2. *Need Step*:
      a. Many people in U.S./on Guam—unhealthy; can lead to chronic health problems.
      b. JoAnna Cruz: bowel disorder; always constipated; required pain medication plus prescription drug to aid movement. Age 35 contracted rheumatoid arthritis with stiffness, inflammation, and deformity of her joints. Diagnosed with Sjogren's Syndrome, diminishing her immune system. Doctor put her on Bactrim for the common flu but it damaged her stomach lining, further harming her digestion. Her ongoing difficulties include physical pain, financial suffering, abbreviated life.
      c. American Journal of Health Promotion (2003): 50-70% of diseases linked to poor health choices. Constipation and colon cancer correlation. Common in America: obesity, heart disease, cancer, diabetes, cataracts, stroke, and hypertension.
      d. Given the ubiquitous Guam fiesta diet + American fast food for college students, increasing computer/video game/ + movie/TV viewing, students exercise little, have a high risk of health problems by their 30's.

C. Satisfaction Step
   1. You should follow the Okinawan Health Program, because it's an easily fulfilled four-week plan, it has a moderate exercise plan, and it can promote longevity.

2. Definition of terms:
   a. Okinawan Health Program: diet and exercise plan developed in Okinawa, emphasizing the principle of caloric density. It recommends that we eat more of the food that has fewer calories in its mass and less food having more calories per volume. Food emphasized includes fresh vegetables, whole grains, fresh fruit, some fish and dairy products, plus moderate aerobic exercise.[see enlarged food chart, plus the FDA food chart for comparison]

3. First, it's an easily fulfilled four-week plan.
   a. Meal planner provides suggested food and serving sizes, automatically calculate number of calories consumed;
   b. Weekly meal plans printed include food shopping list—foods readily found in grocery stores or Simply Food in Agana Heights: brown rice, beans, whole grains, noodles, fresh vegetables, fruit, soy bean products (tofu, milk, miso soup), some fish and cheese, and a sparse amount of vegetable oils and low-sodium condiments.
   c. Drink water (8 glasses/day) and tea; if alcohol drunk be moderate; avoid or minimize sugared soft and other drinks.
   d. Amounts: can eat as much as desired of some foods, especially apples, berries, and peaches, broccoli, squash, green peas, and fat-free yogurt and tofu. White flaky fish, brown rice, pasta, sushi, and cooked beans can be eaten in medium-sized portions a few times per day.

   Overall, can eat a sufficient or greater amount of the right kind of food with fewer calories. Feel full, fulfilled, with the amount of food eaten and the high protein foods that decrease hunger. Maintain healthy body weight, and if overweight, lose weight. If stress a carb diet, this promotes the correct ones—foods like vegetables, fruit, whole grains, and other unprocessed foods in their natural state. Look younger, have increased energy to get through the day. Food plan is self-fulfilling.

4. Next, it has a moderate exercise plan
   a. initial weigh in and BMI determined.
   b. plan provides list of different physical activities and intensity levels paired with calories consumed in its calorie burning chart. [see chart]
   c. 2 criteria in the plan: aerobic fitness and flexibility. Aerobic strengthens the heart. Flexibility exercises a secret to feeling and looking young. [additional information included here]

Once burned calories calculated, should see deficit in total calories burned per day. With fewer calories consumed/day and more burned up with exercising, excessive body fat consumed.

5. Lastly, it can promote longevity
   Yes, food has to be eaten to live, but food in the Okinawan Health Program provides benefits beyond survival.
   a. promotes longer life through its healing power
   b. can reverse medical problems.

   25-year study of dietary habits in Okinawa show impressive health benefits for the people there. All else being equal, a healthier person lives longer. [additional information included here]

6. Internal summary: The Okinawan Health Plan will add years to your life and life to your years since it's an easily fulfilled four-week plan, it has a moderate exercise plan, and it can promote longevity.

D. Visualization Step
   1. Those following the Okinawan Health Plan will experience a feeling of vitality and wellness.
      a. yearly physicals will have low scores in typical problem areas like cholesterol, sodium, blood pressure, sugar levels, and BMI
      b. 50-year olds the physical and mental health age of a 35-year old — not over the hill. Many on this health program to live into 90's and 100's.

   2. If you do not change your eating habits from this [see chart of No Optional Foods—typical fast food, fiesta diet items] then your medical health care cost will be very expensive, will make your physicians and clinic/s very wealthy over next 40-50 years (if you live that long).

E. Action Step
   Recommend taking baby steps towards changing eating and exercising habits:

   1. Just say no to all fast food places like Wendy's, McDonald's, Kentucky Fried Chicken, etc. Eat at Subway or Taco Bell, if you must. Subway: tuna sandwich. Avoid mayo, oil, and meat. Taco Bell: only bean burrito without cheese, can ask for extra lettuce and tomatoes.

2. Little by little, decrease meat intake, especially pork and beef. Eat just lean chicken (not fried) and turkey provided at many fiestas. Later, wean from chicken and turkey, too. You will notice that your taste buds will change, your meat cravings will diminish.

3. On campus, park car at furthest end of parking lot to get one-half hour a day of walking. Try the far side of Field House for walk to the EC building. KMart or Payless: park furthest spot on lot. Over time, will not seem a big deal and weight will drop, little by little.

4. Purposefully start walking 15 minutes/day apart from walking from car to buildings. After a few weeks, increase to 30 minutes, then 45, and eventually 1 hour everyday or every other day.

5. If have a dog, run with them circling your residence. My dog tries to get me to run even faster.

6. Do aerobic exercises daily, such as: dancing, jumping jacks, running.. Start with 15 minutes/day, 2-4 days per week, then increase to one-half hour for 1 month, every other day.
Later, increase it to 1 hour every other day.

You may feel healthy now because you are youthful, but if you are eating improperly your body is slowly breaking down. Consider these baby steps towards a happier, healthier life.

PERSUASIVE SPEECH EVALUATION FORM

_____ Persuasion Speech Evaluation

_____

(name)	Time (6-8 minutes)
1. Attention Step (gained attention, orientation to topic, credibility)	0 1 2 3 4
2. Need Step (statement, illustration, ramification, pointing—harms) a. b. c. d.	0 1 2 3 4
3. Satisfaction Step: Proposition (clear, appropriate, w/3 supporting points)	0 1 2 3 4
Satisfaction Step (reasons/plan clear, points coherent, organized, unified) Definition/s:	0 1 2 3 4
Development (logical support: specific, relevant, sufficient, valid) a. b. c. Transitions used between points _____ other _____ Internal summary of proposition plus points	0 1 2 3 4 0 1 2 3 4 0 1 2 3 4
4. Visualization Step: benefits of reasons, practicality of plan a. Positive b. Negative	0 1 2 3 4

5. Action Step: specific actions, vivid, final appeal, voice finality
  a.
  b.	

Eye contact and appropriate use of notes	0 1 2 3 4
Delivery: phrasing, loudness, rate, pronunciation	0 1 2 3 4
Subject Selection: analysis—audience/occasion	0 1 2 3 4
Visual Aid: helpful purpose, used effectively	0 1 2 3 4
Fit time limit (6-8 minutes) or not?	

[0-inadequate, 1-adequate, 2-good, 3-very good, 4-excellent] Grade _____

REFERENCES

1. M. Horinouchi. Unpublished speech/University of Guam, Mangilao, Guam. Feb. 3, 2005.

2. Ehninger, D., Gronbeck, R., McKerrow, R., and Monroe, A. *Principles and Types of Speech Communication*, 10th ed. Glenview, IL: Scott, Foresman and Company, 1986.

3. M. Horinouchi. Unpublished speech/University of Guam, Mangilao, Guam. Feb. 21, 2005.

4. Gronbeck, B., German, K., Ehninger, D, & Monroe, A. *Principles of Speech Communication*, 12th Brief ed. Boston: HarperCollins College Publishers, 1995.

5. M. Horinouchi. Unpublished speech/University of Guam, Mangilao, Guam. Mar. 10, 2005.

6. M. Horinouchi. Unpublished speech/University of Guam, Mangilao, Guam. Mar. 29, 2005.

7. M. Horinouchi. Unpublished speech/University of Guam, Mangilao, Guam. Apr. 19, 2005.

8. M. Horinouchi. Unpublished speech/University of Guam, Mangilao, Guam. May 5, 2005.

Sample Syllabus

PUBLIC SPEAKING SPRING 2006
Time:
Instructor:
Office, Hours:
Phone, Email:
Text: *Public Speaking Basics*

Jan. 18 Introduction.
    20 Ch.1 Communicating in Public; H/W #1 due.

Jan. 23 Ch.2 Anxiety About Speaking; H/W 2.
    25 Ch.3 Delivering the Speech ; H/W 3.
    27 Speech 1 preparation, video examples. See Appendix A.

Jan. 30 Video examples of vocal delivery in speeches.
Feb. 1 *Speech 1* Memorable Moment (2-3 minutes).
    3 Ch.4 Subject Selection and Audience Analysis.

Feb 6 Ch.4 Subject Selection and Audience Analysis; H/W 4 (to be copied for next class).
    8 Ch.5 Creating a Main Idea: thesis sentence exercises.
    10 Ch.5 Thesis sentences (continuation); H/W #5 Thesis due next class.

Feb. 13 Speech 2 prep incorporating the *Need Step* p.57, 59, video examples. H/W 5.

15   Ch.6 Motivational Appeals.
     Ch.6 Motivation Appeals—Needs; problem outcomes in various phenomena; H/W 6.

Feb. 20   *Speech 2* Criticism Speech (2-3 minutes) Submit list of suffering noted in the speech.
          Videotape: View and critique your Speech 2 this week, submit Friday as H/W 6b.
     22   Ch.7 Organizing and Outlining the Speech; exercises
     24   Ch.7 Organizing and Outlining, transitions; H/W 6b (critique), H/W 7

Feb. 27   Ch.8 Introductions and Conclusions; exercise; H/W 8
Mar. 1   Ch.9 Supporting and Amplifying Your Ideas
      3   Speech 3 prep, video examples. *Must have H/W 13* bio of yourself for distribution.

Mar. 6   Ch.9 Supporting and Amplifying exercises; H/W 9 . *Verify your Speech 3 person.*
      8   *Speaking Persuasively* (video) to be shown in class
     10   *Speech 3* Speech of Introduction (2-3 minutes)
          Videotape: View and critique your Speech 3 next week, submit next Friday as H/W 9b.

Mar. 13   Ch.10 Informative Speeches, patterns.
     15   Critique sample outlines; H/W 10.
     17   Speech 4 prep, video examples. H/W 11: *Informative Speech outline* (1st draft) *due.*

Mar. 20   Ch.9 review: using visual aids, Informative Speech outline due.
     22   Speech 4 Informative Speech video examples, review Ch. 7 Transitions (*in* speech)..
     24   Speech 4 Informative Speech (continued). Verify your outlines are reviewed.

Mar. 27   *Speech 4* Informative Speech (6-8 minutes). Submit final draft of H/W 11 (outline).
     29   *Speech 4* Informative Speech Submit final draft of H/W 11 (outline)..
     31   Ch.11 Wording the Speech; H/W 12

Apr. 3 Ch.12 Special Occasion Speeches, Speech 5 video examples
5 Ch.12 Special Occasion Speeches, Speech 5 video examples
7 Ch.14 Speeches to Persuade. Research Persuasive Speech topic, outline over break.

April 10-15 Easter Week.

Apr. 17 *Speech 5* Speech of Good Will or to Entertain (2.5-5 minutes). Videotape.
View and critique your Speech 5 on video for an extra credit homework assignment.
19 *Speech 5* (continue as needed). Videotape. Speech 6 video examples to be shown.
21 H/W 15: Audience Analysis questionnaire for your Sp.6 topic due, with copies for the entire class to fill out this day during class. Submit even if you are not present.

Apr. 24 Ch.13 Listening; H/W #14. Work on H/W 16 Persuasive Speech outline.
26 Ch.14 Persuasive Speeches; H/W 16 Persuasive Speech outline due for review.
28 Ch.14 Persuasive Speeches, video examples; review Persuasive Speech outlines.

May 1 Persuasive Speech video examples.
3 *Speech 6* (6-8 minutes, use a detailed outline only). Submit final draft of H/W 16.
5 *Speech 6.*   Submit final draft of H/W 16.

May 8 Review for Final Exam.
10 Part 1 of exam.
12 Part 2 of exam.

* I must be contacted before or at the scheduled speech times if they will be missed, *to be completed the following class (if time) or on your return to class.* There is no guarantee of being able to make up speeches. If lateness is unexcused and you are allowed to make up a speech, the speech will be marked off 1 full grade. Assignments not completed, for whatever reason, will receive an F. Homework needs to be done on time since answers will be given out during class.

Grading (subject to change)   *Grading Example*

Speech 1:	5%	b: 3 * .05= .15	A: 3.5-4.0
2:	8%	b+: 3.35 * .08= .268	B: 2.5-3.49
3:	8%	b-: 2.65 * .08= .212	C: 1.5-2.49
4:	18%	a: 4 * .18= .72	D: 1.0-1.49
5:	8%	c: 2 * .08= .16	F: 0.0- .99
6:	18%	a+: 4.35 * .18= .783	
Exam:	18%	a-: 3.65 * .18= .657	
Homework:	12%	c-: 1.65 * .12= .198	
Attendance:	5%	a: 4 * .05= .2	

total: 3.348 = B+ (final grade)

A. COURSE CONTENT: A study of speech planning and preparation, choosing subjects and recognizing purposes, analyzing audiences and occasions, thesis sentences, basic appeals, developing and supporting ideas, beginning and ending speeches, use of language, visual aids, voice, and gestures, organizational patterns & outlining, and the common types of speeches delivered.

B. TEACHING METHODS: Lecture, discussion, video instruction, class exercises.

C. LEARNING OBJECTIVES FOR STUDENTS: Students will demonstrate knowledge of:

1. speech planning, purposes, and goals
2. subject selection, research, and controlling speech anxiety
3. creating thesis sentences, writing introductions and conclusions, and organizing a variety of speeches
4. logical support of their ideas, transitional words, and use of appropriate visual aids
5. effective language usage and delivery techniques
6. the creating of a variety of speeches, including the principles and types of informative and persuasive speeches
7. listener motivation and speaker credibility

Homework Assignments

HOMEWORK ASSIGNMENTS

Ch.1 homework: Likes and Dislikes of speakers and/or speeches

Ch.2 homework: List 2 recommendations for controlling stage fright

Ch.3 homework: List 5 words of which you are unsure of the pronunciation

Ch.4 homework: list 3 most common characteristics shared by the class and what relevance these have (in general) for speeches ; list 3 topics which you consider inappropriate subject matter for class speeches and explain why

Ch.5 homework: Thesis sentences

Ch.6 homework: (a) clip and bring to class 1 newspaper or magazine advertisement, noting the motivational appeals being used, briefly explain why you think the appeals were selected, and do you think they are effective

(b) which motivational appeals would you use to convince a friend to stay in school, and why?

Ch.7 homework: prepare a 1 page biography of yourself (accurate or fantasy or both) homework: choosing 1 of the topics listed, organize main supporting points for it following one of the outlining methods provided

Ch.8 homework: determine the types of Introductions and Conclusions used in the sample speech provided.

Ch.9 homework: find the type of supporting methods used in the sample speech.

Ch.10 homework: given the topics provided, create specific purposes for informative and persuasive speeches; create an Informative Speech outline.

Ch.11 homework: list a slogan, describe the imagery it evokes, a metaphor used by the group involved, and your guess as to the effectiveness of these.

Ch.12 homework: provide a biography of yourself (accurate or inaccurate, as desired).

Ch.13 homework: (a) is there anything wrong with not listening to a boring speaker?

(b) can faking attention be harmful? Why/why not?

Ch.14 homework: prepare a questionnaire about your Persuasion Speech topic for class response; create a Persuasive Speech outline.

Sample Test Study Guide

PUBLIC SPEAKING FINAL TEST STUDY GUIDE

PART I (First day of exam)

Chapter 1: Important public function public speaking serves; individual function it serves.

Chapter 2: Techniques that can be used to minimize or control speech anxiety.

Chapter 3: Pros and cons of the different methods of delivery.

Chapter 4: General purposes and specific purposes. Choosing a topic: Factors that influence the choice. Audience analysis: Explanation, variables to consider, and their use.

Chapter 6: Motivation appeals explanation, common needs, using motivational needs.

Chapter 7: Organizational patterns: What they are, how they're arranged/prepared [chronological, spatial, topical, problem-solution, causal].

Motivated Sequence.

Transitions: What they are, where they're primarily used, examples.

Chapter 8: Introductions and Conclusions: Functions, common faults, methods.

Chapter 9: Supporting and Amplifying ideas: Purpose, methods.

Presentational support material: purpose, questions for use, rules for using.

Chapter 10: Motivated Sequence: Need Step explanation.

Chapter 11: Wording: Guidelines for language use.

Chapter 13: Listening: Necessary orientation of the speaker, suggestions for listening to a Speech.

Chapter 14: Persuasion: General purpose, transferring the message into needs, people changing (p. 70, Motivated Sequence for the Persuasive Speech.

PART II (Second day of exam)

Chapter 5: Main idea/thesis: What it is, characteristics, points supporting the thesis. Like the thesis homework, be prepared to identify mistakes and rewrite poor theses.

Chapter 10: Outlining Informative Speech: Be prepared to create an informative speech outline from a list of topics to be provided, just like the Informative Speech one. All of the words originally on the outline form will be omitted so you will fill them in, as well.

Chapter 14: Persuasion: Building credibility, responding to the audience's general Predispositions.

Optional Demonstration Speech

DEMONSTRATION SPEECH

Create a 5-6 minute demonstration speech following the guidelines presented below. Surprisingly, many students do not practice or time themselves in advance. Speeches over six minutes will be stopped and the student will be graded on what was presented up to that point, as well as for what was not completed. If there is class time and it is apparent that the student will finish shortly after 6 minutes, the speech *may* be allowed to continue but will be graded lower for being overtime. The instructor will not be a timekeeper for the student. This is excellent time management practice for the business world outside of school.

Guidelines

Throughout their lives, people tell and show others how to do things. While it may appear simple and matter-of-fact to show someone how to do something, effective teachers are not that common, whether it be demonstrating how to prepare a certain dish of food, how to troubleshoot a car problem and then how to fix it, how to assemble various products, how to sell innumerable products or services, and so on. Thus, demonstration speeches are a necessary and common type of informative speech that follows a chronological, process order in the body of the speech.

In this speech you physically show and explain to your audience how to do something. You have to *do something* and talk about how to do it while you do it. For example, bring the ingredients to class and *make the cake.*

For such a speech at work, you will need to have all the necessary supplies and equipment. This speech also emphasizes the use of introductions and conclusions, organization, transitions, physical movement, and verbal descriptions.

The time allowed for this speech in a classroom setting may be only *5-6 minutes* so you cannot do something that is complicated or time consuming. It is possible that you may select a process that can have separate stages partially completed at home that can be individually completed in class, showing how each stage is done. Subject selection is crucial for fitting the time limit. There should be no 4 minute or 7 minute speeches if 5-6 minutes is the parameter. Your grade will be lowered for being too short or too long. Be sure to time yourself at home to ensure you can do the demonstration plus the introduction and conclusion in time allotted.

As noted above, you will need to bring all the necessary presentational aids to the speaking site (e.g., class), such as the object(s) you will be using and necessary tools to complete the task. Extension cords, tape, cutting boards, and special surfaces may be needed. Ensure the objects and tools used are all large enough to be seen by the entire audience (class). For demonstration purposes you may need to also have and use substitute equipment and/or supplies to ensure that everyone can see everything.

You should expect to follow a *time pattern* in organizing and delivering your demonstration, beginning with the first step in the process and continuing through the last one. Be clear about the sequence so you do not have to backtrack or entirely omit an important step in the process. As you go from step to step, use transitions such as: *first ...., second ...., third .... for the next step ...., as you can see...., also consider...., not only ... but also ....,* and so on.

To aid you in your organization, follow the steps below:

A. *Introduction.* The purpose of the introduction is to get the audience's attention and orient them to the topic. Begin by describing a situation in which your listeners can visualize wanting and needing to know how to do the process you are about to demonstrate. *Do not begin your speech with*: "Today I'm going to show you how to make a ____." This is boring. Create an interesting scenario here with your verbal description to gain the listeners' attention and convey the speech topic. Consider something like: "Last Saturday I was swimming at ____ Beach with a friend, enjoying the cool, gentle waves, the warming sun, the laughter of kids on the beach, when all of a sudden ...." After finishing this scenario, state the purpose of the speech: "If you are ever in this situation, you will want to know how to ...." or " ... so today I will be demonstrating how to ...." Added to this, state the reasons for wanting to know how to do what will be demonstrated.

B. *Body*. At this point, go through the steps in the process, showing the class how to do each one. This is not simply an informative speech in which you tell us how to do something. You have to actually show the class how, describing each step in the process. If the speech is about 6 minutes long, you should expect the body of the speech to be about 4 minutes long.

1. Begin with an overview. Give a general description of what you expect to do. Be concise.
2. Describe and point to the objects to be used. Define any key terms, materials, and/or equipment the audience will not know.
3. Start with the 1st step in the process. Be sure to explain *how* and *why* to do each action and clearly show this to the audience.
4. 2nd step
5. and so on through the last step These steps should take from 3.5-4 minutes to complete.

If you are doing something that you have described and still need to continue doing it a little longer (such as some final mixing) you may have time to describe the process at work, the history behind it, or some other interesting fact. Your grade will be lowered if you are silent at any point.

C. *Conclusion*. The purpose of the conclusion is to wrap up the speech and then end. The speech is not over when the last step is completed. Do not say "That's it" and simply hold up the completed object. There is a 3-part conclusion. First, summarize the key steps in the process. Second, remind the audience of the good reasons for doing the activity. Third, close with a final thought.

Further Comments

Be organized. Have materials ready to use when you set them out before you begin the speech. Quickly set them up or your grade may be lowered. Do not waste class time writing on the chalkboard—do it in advance or even on poster paper. Again, verify your audience can clearly see the objects, tools, and process of demonstration. You may need larger-sized substitutes. Bring towels to clean up any mess. Do not use something noisy like an osterizer to make crushed ice since it is so loud your speaking will not be heard (you have to continually speak). Have the ice already crushed. Businesses have time constraints, as well, so people at work do not want to sit around while you get ready and if you are unorganized.

Examples of suitable topics (verify with your teacher): food dishes like cakes, cookies, lumpia, corn soup, fried bananas; financial topics like balancing a checkbook, filling out a tax form, completing a loan application; physical health topics like basic exercises, weight lifting, stretching; physical hobbies like dancing, massage, self-defense; arts & crafts topics like paper mache flowers, soap balls, knitting/ crocheting, or homemade greeting cards; emergency procedures like CPR, the Heimlich maneuver, or tourniquet; humorous topics such as cheating on tests, getting out of a driving ticket, how to drop a boy/girlfriend, brain surgery; and so on.

Examples of topics that have been failures in class. Avoid these: computer use, playing a guitar, card games, female facial make-up, and the origami crane. This demonstration speech *is not a performance*, so do not sing to the class, play a guitar song, etc.

Examples of products not allowed: anything with alcohol or tobacco in it (against school rules).

Using visual aids. This was covered in Chapter 9 so review their use there. They are used to gain attention, maintain interest, and both clarify and reinforce the speaker's ideas. They can make the supporting facts clearer, more vivid, and convincing. Remember, you should only use one if you determine it is necessary for the process to be understood and completed.

SAMPLE DEMONSTRATION SPEECH:
CLAM CHOWDER

[Set-up before the speech actually begins: ensure the table is arranged to suit this speech. Everything should be open or unwrapped, ready to use, and placed on the side of the table. Do not leave the finished product in sight. For cost and ease of demonstrating, the speaker may reduce all of the amounts by about one-fourth (e.g., 1 potato). The speaker should pre-cook the separate ingredients since this can't be done in 5-6 minutes, using these to actually put together later in the speech. Clear, glass-type cooking pots allow the audience to see how something is cooking and mixed. Be prepared, think through every step.]

A. Introduction

It was a cool evening as I headed home after work, wondering what to fix my family for dinner. What would be different, something we usually only get at special times at restaurants? Clam chowder! I can make it on 30 minutes, it's a meal in itself, it tastes better and is cheaper than what is served in restaurants, and apart from a few items, it is healthy. I always keep the ingredients on hand except for the cream so I just need to stop at the store to buy that.

B. Body

1. In the kitchen, assemble the ingredients and implements on the countertop and stove: 3-6 oz. cans minced clams, 1-6 oz. bottle clam juice, 4 oz. frozen sliced bacon, 1 medium onion, 4 cloves fresh garlic or 2 tsp. minced garlic, 4 medium russet potatoes, 3-8" carrots, 2-12" stalks celery, 3-8" zucchini, ¼ tsp. salt, ¼ tsp. black pepper, ¼ tsp. celery seed (if not, dill), 1 Tbl. olive oil, 1-4 oz. stick butter, 16 oz. heavy (whip) cream, cutting board and knife, medium pot, vegetable steamer, large pot, can opener, medium size stirring spoon, and soup ladle.
[speaker should not place any items or equipment across the front of the table which will later block the audience's view of the preparation]

2. Place vegetable steamer basket into medium pot, fill with water to cover the 3 legs, place on the stove at high heat. Wash potatoes, carrots, and celery (no peeling). Vegetables will be cut small to increase the likelihood when later eaten that they will be mixed in with clams. Cut the potatoes into 3/8" cubes, place in steamer, cut carrots in 1/8" pieces and place atop potatoes, covering with the lid. When water comes to a boil, reduce heat to medium and tilt lid slightly.
[speaker should scrub 1 potato and carrot, explaining how and why as cutting both of them; rinse. Place these into the steamer and pretend to cook. Have some of each in a baggie already cut and precooked that you can later poke with a toothpick to show just done.]

3. Large pot: put olive oil in the bottom, slice and chop frozen bacon slices into ¼" pieces and place in pot, turn on high heat, slice onion in ¼" by ¼" pieces and put atop bacon, reduce to medium heat, add finely chopped garlic to spread out its flavor, stir so bacon doesn't stick and burn. Remove from heat when onion is translucent. Add butter, cut up into 4 separate pieces.
[speaker should slice and chop just 2 sections of bacon and onions, explaining how and why they are done that way, then put pre-cooked bacon, onion, garlic, and melted butter into pot]

4. Slice each zucchini and celery lengthwise in 4 equal pieces, chop zucchini cross-ways in 3/16" pieces and set aside, chop celery in 1/8 in pieces and set aside.
[speaker should slice 1 each zucchini and celery, and only chop 1" of each for demo purposes]

5. Check doneness of potatoes and carrots with a toothpick, remove from heat when barely done, scoop out and add (without the steamer water) to the big pot, on top of the butter/onions/garlic/ bacon.
[speaker should poke 1 each piece of pre-cooked potato and carrot to show doneness]

6. Open the cans of minced clams and drain the juice only into the large pot. Add the bottle of clam juice, the zucchini, and the spices. [speaker should have the cans opened before the speech begin and at this time pretend to slightly open one. The speaker may use a can of tuna in place of costlier clams, draining the tuna water into the pot, and use water instead of costlier real clam juice, labeling a small bottle of water as "clam juice."]

7. Turn on the heat under the large pot to low, stir all the contents to mix thoroughly. Cook for 3 minutes, stirring constantly, just enough to cook the zucchini a little and mix all the flavors.
[speaker will do this for about 5 seconds]

8. With the contents warm, add the finely chopped celery and cream and stir thoroughly. The celery will add a little crunch in addition to its taste and nutrition. Stir intermittently for 3 minutes, just to warm the cream. Do not allow this to boil for the cream will curdle.
[speaker may add milk for demonstration purposes]

9. Add the clams and stir thoroughly for one minute. Remove from heat. Cooking the clams too much can give them a rubbery texture.
[speaker may add the drained tuna for demonstration purposes]

10. Serve with a soup ladle in a soup bowl.
[speaker should ladle some into a bowl for the audience to see]

C. Conclusion

In summary, assemble all the necessary ingredients, tools, and cookware. Wash and cut up the potatoes, carrot, zucchini, and celery, steam the potatoes and carrots in one pot, cut up the bacon, onion, and garlic, placing them in oil in a large pot to sauté, add butter to the sauté, put the cooked potatoes and carrots on top of them, add the clam juice, zucchini, and spices, stir to mix, cook slightly, stir in the celery and cream, cook slightly, add the clams, cook slightly, then remove from heat.

This is a delicious substitute for the local favorite, corn soup. It is inexpensive, quick, easy, and nutritious, given all the vegetables. Outside the canned clams, clam juice, and heavy cream—which are available at many stores, most people already have all of the items at home.

Instead of the Friday Night Seafood Buffet at the Hilton, consider the Friday Night Chowder at Cruz's House of Clams.

SAMPLE DEMONSTRATION
SPEECH EVALUATION FORM

_____ Demonstration Speech

_____

(name)   Time (5-6 minutes)

Introduction: Gained attention, orientation to topic • interesting illustration/scenario (yes/no) • purpose of the demonstration clear (yes/no) • reason/s given for needing to know (yes/no)	0 1 2 3 4
Visual Aids/materials to be used were described, large enough, not hidden, properly referred to	0 1 2 3 4
Demonstration was organized, 1st step to last	0 1 2 3 4
Conclusion: Summary of steps + reasons for knowing/doing Future use; voice conveyed a sense of finality	0 1 2 3 4
This _was_ a _demonstration_ speech — subject selection	0 1 2 3 4
Expect the audience to be able to now do it	0 1 2 3 4
Eye contact: spoke to the audience, not to the aid	0 1 2 3 4
Phrasing: spoke with complete phrases	0 1 2 3 4
Inarticulate sounds/filler words (um/ur/and uh/OK/etc)	0 1 2 3 4
Pauses: enough, correct length, no extended silences	0 1 2 3 4
Loudness: all was heard, varied, no fading out	0 1 2 3 4
Pronunciation (if a criteria)	0 1 2 3 4
Overall time (5-6 minutes) if too long, how much grade is lowered if too short, how much grade is lowered	

Grading scale: 0-inadequate, 1-adequate, 2-good, 3-very good, 4-excellent Grade _____

Standard American English Sounds

STANDARD AMERICAN ENGLISH SOUNDS[1]

ē : east, need, he

ĭ : if, pit

ā : ate, cake, great (used as the pronunciation for the alphabet letter *a*, *a* quality/grade, in reference to the musical scale, for some business names, or for special stress)

ĕ : ever, get, thread

ă : ask, pat, laugh

ä : arm, father, spa (interchangeable sound with ¼ below)

ŏ : object, body, cot (shaped with a rounded mouth)

ô : off, cloth, caught (shaped with a pronounced oblong mouth)

ō : oak, hope, photo

ŏŏ : cook, should, cushion

o͞o : do, you, tooth, true

ûr : urge, irk, work prefer (in single-syllable words or stressed syllables)

   (interchangeable sound)

ər : surprise, perfume, actor, color (in unstressed syllables)

ŭ : of, ugly, blood, enough (in single-syllable words or stressed syllables)

(interchangeable sound; this the pronunciation for almost uses of the article *a*)

ə : above, system, arena (in unstressed syllables)

ī : I, guide, height, my

oi : oil, noise, joy

ou : out, brown, how

p : paper, open, lip

b : ball, table, job

t : time, after, fact

d : day, body, tired

k : cat, equal, work

g : give, begin, dig (most *g*'s are pronounced like a *j* or a *zh*)

f : fact, left, tough (voiceless sound)

v : very, oven, of (voiced)

th : thin, method, with (voiceless; force out more air around the tongue, teeth, and lips)

th : the, other, smooth (less forced air, voiced sound; *th* is used before words beginning with a vowel (*th* air), *th*... is used before words beginning with a consonant (*th*... pie).

s : slip, last, place (voiceless; many *s*'s are pronounced like a *z*)

z : zero, easy, news (voiced)

sh : she, fiction, fish (voiceless)

zh : decision, beige, vision (many *s* and *ge* letters have this sound) h : hair, unhurt (voiceless; blow air out; a few *h*'s are silent, as in *honor*)

hw : why, which, nowhere (voiceless; blow out air for the initial *h* part)

w : with, equal, language (voiced; some *w*'s are pronounced *hw*)

ch : chin, future, such (voiceless; distinguish between this and a *tr* sound)

j : job, engine, stage (voiced; note *ge*, *dge* letters having this sound)

y : yes, unit, lawyer (voiced; note many *u* letters having this sound)

r : rain, arm, far (voiced; note difference between *ur* and *r* sounds)

l : lid, salt, feel (voiced)

m : man, rims, warm (voiced, through nasal cavity)

n : no, and, seen (voiced, through nasal cavity)

ng : angle, singer, song (voiced, through nasal cavity, avoid making an *n* sound)

îr : pier, fear, weird

âr : care, lair, swear

REFERENCE

1. American Heritage Dictionary of the English Language (3rd ed.). Boston, MA: Houghton Mifflin Company, 1992).

Vocal Variation Exercises

VOCAL VARIATION EXERCISES1

A. *Rate of Speech and Meaning*

1. In combination with the actual words being said, the rate of speech provides a clue of the meaning being suggested by the speaker. Notice how the speed (fast or slow) at which the following are said affects the meaning. [students to take turns saying the following]

   Meaning?
   a. Pay the man. (Fast)   _____
   b. Oh, I guess so. (Slow)   _____
   c. Are you for real? (Slow)   _____
   d. You don't know that. (Fast)   _____
   e. Give it to me now. (Slow)   _____

2. Pauses between words and phrases alter the implied meaning, as well. [students to read the following, altering where they pause, then comment on the changes in meaning]

   Meaning?
   a. Only you can prevent forest fires.   _____
   b. He who laughs last laughs loudest.   _____
   c. The only wish I have is to serve my country. _____

B. *Volume of Sound*: Degree of Loudness.

    1. Read the following sentences, providing a loudness stress for the words italicized.

a. I said, *clean up* your *room*.	e. *Run* a little faster.
b. *Hit me* with another card.	f. You *missed* it.
c. Can we *go* now?	g. Can't you *speak up*?
d. *Put on the brakes*.	h. Don't go. *Don't go*.

    2. From your experience, what volume levels are likely used by people in these professions?

        Volume level: loud, medium, quiet
        a. Waitress   _____
        b. Professional wrestler   _____
        c. Anxious, scared person   _____
        d. High school teacher   _____
        e. Disk jockey playing top 100 songs   _____
        f. Artist   _____
        g. Doctor's office secretary   _____
        h. Church helper, in church   _____

    3. Read the following sentences in different volume levels to indicate the personality/profession.

        a. Oh, look at the reddish-purple sunset.
        b. Please, hear me out.
        c. You mustn't go.
        d. I'm so upset I could scream.
        e. There is so much left unsaid between us.

C. *Pitch Changes*

1. Read the following by changing your pitch between words (step shifts): higher, middle, lower.

   a. Give it to me ^{right} now.

   b. You're a ^{good} dog.

   c. I _{need a cold drink.}

   d. ^{She} is some _{cook}.

   e. You fly can a kite.

2. Read the following words using an appropriate inflection (a pitch change up or down within a word) according to the expected meaning listed at the right.

Word Meaning expected

a. Wait	Question
b. Maybe	Question
c. Maybe	Probably not
d. Oh, oh, oh.	You've got to be kidding.
e. Stop it.	Are you sure?
f. I said so.	I'm the boss.
g. Who else:	Nobody but you
h. So	So what?
i. I will.	Surprise
j. Stand up.	Angry command
k. You're the one.	You're guilty.
l. Goodbye	Finality
m. Here we go.	All over again

D. *Stress* (Could result from loudness, pitch, and/or duration emphasis, and include vocal tone).

1. For the pairs of words below, given a vocal stress to one word, then to the other, for different meanings. Example: I am. Stressing the *I* means only me. Stressing *am* means affirmative.

	Meaning 1	Meaning 2
a. Come on.		
b. Get out.		
c. Keep out.		
d. So long.		
e. How much?		
f. Help me.		
g. Tell me.		
h. Fry the burgers.		

2. Stress the italicized word in each sentence below. After saying it aloud, explain its meaning.

Then, choose another word to stress and explain the difference in meaning.

a. Is *that* the person?

b. You are a *good* dog.

c. He has a nice *car*.

d. Shouldn't *we* go now?

e. Maybe. I said *maybe*.

f. Baby, the *rain* must fall.

g. Don't *wait* for me.

h. *I* want a pizza.

1. Adapted from Creative Dramatics in the Classroom, *The Center for Learning*, 1997.